BEPPO

CLO\...

A story for children written for grownups to read

By Max Robinson

Author's Note:

Allow me to introduce you to Beppo. Beppo was a string puppet I played with when I was about seven years old. My friends also had puppets, together we put on shows for our class at school to watch. Our lovely class teacher was Miss Hudson who made a stage for Beppo and his friends to perform on.

One night, around sixty-eight years after his last performance Beppo entered a dream while I was deeply asleep. He told me he wanted to perform again and asked me to write the scripts for him. These scripts are stories for children but for grownups to read if that makes any sense.

The picture above is Beppo's descendant from Amazon. He is sitting beside me as I write and will be throughout all of the adventures we are about to share.

So Beppo, I am ready to start if you are.

Off we go. Oh and by the way that's me below, photograph taken at the time when Beppo and I were playing together. Oh and by the way for a second time, my name is David I write under the pen-name of Max Robinson but in the story David I will be. Now we really can *Off we go*.
Max

BEPPO THE CLOWN: A story for children written for grownups to read
Beppo's life had been long but it was a long time since it had been fun. For as far back as he could remember Beppo had lived in a cupboard away from being able to play. Each time the door opened he hoped things were going to change and turn back to the way they used to be but that was never the case. The cupboard door would close and a new long time begin.

But that is not what happened on this day. The door opened a hand reached in and took hold of Beppo but before he could start to be happy he was put into a black plastic bag where he feared his long life would soon be no longer. Actually that is not what happened.

"Look Mummy, isn't he cute ?"

"You're too old for teddy bears," Mummy replied.

"He's not a teddy bear, he's a puppet, he's a clown."

"My name is Beppo," Beppo said but only one person in the charity shop heard him speak.

"And my name is David," David whispered back before quite loudly asking his mother if he could have the toy.

"How much is he ?" David's Mummy asked the lady behind the shop counter.

"Fifty pence."

Fifty pence ? Fifty pennies ? That was a funny way of saying four shillings and tuppence, Beppo considered. Funny but not amusing, certainly not for a clown. Twelve pennies to the shilling, four shillings were made up of forty-eight pennies needing two more large dark brown coins to add up to fifty.

"I've got that much in my pocket," David said to his mother, "can I buy him ?"

"Go on then."

Beppo was about to start a new and very long life, a new and very long happy life.

"What's your favourite thing to eat ?" Beppo asked David with David being again the only one in the shop who could hear him.

"Chocolates," he replied.

"So they are for me. Once you have sucked the chocolate inside the sweet there is an adventure."

"I've got a box of chocolates at home, let's go and have an adventure."

"Or perhaps two adventures."

"Even three, no make that six !"

The Yo-Yo:
"There was a farmer had a dog," Beppo began to sing, "and BINGO was his name oh. B-I-N-G-O, B-I-N-G-O and BINGO was his name oh."

David knew the song even if it was something for children slightly younger than he was, he and Beppo started to sing a duo.

"There was a farmer had a dog and BINGO was his name oh. B-I-N-G-O, B-I-N-G-O and BINGO was his name oh."

"Now here's a version for you and for me," Beppo smiled. "There was a David had a friend and BEPPO was his name oh. B-E-P-P-O, B-E-P-P-O and BEPPO was his name oh. Come on David sing it with me."

David of course obliged. "There was a David had a friend and BEPPO was his name oh. B-E-P-P-O, B-E-P-P-O and BEPPO was his name oh."

"Time for our first adventure," Beppo's clown hair sparkled and his nose glowed deep red. "What chocolate have you got we can eat ?"

"How about a Yo-Yo."

"A scrummy, yummy mint chocolate biscuit."

(Yo-Yo biscuits were discontinued in the year two thousand and three but that made no difference to David and Beppo's adventure.)

"What tricks can you play with a yo-yo ?"

"You are the clown, you show me."

Beppo rolled the yo-yo down its string a few times then spun it up into the air and round in a circle before yo-yoing up and down again.

"That is called circling the world. This is taking a dog for a walk."

The yo-yo went up and down before Beppo allowed it to roll along the ground a bit like a dog on a lead.

"That's taking a dog for a walk."

Obviously.

"Heart of oak are our ships," the lady said. "Today ships are made of metal but their hearts are all still made of Oak. Thank you Nipper for coming here today."

Apparently she could see Nipper but David and Beppo were invisible to her.

"This little oak tree was planted," she continued, "here in Windsor Castle yesterday, Tuesday the twentieth of June eighteen thirty-seven to mark my coronation"

The lady speaking was not a lady, she was Her Majesty Queen Victoria.

"If you would now christen my Coronation Windsor Oak Tree that would be really nice."

Nipper obliged.

"Thank you. Thank you for that royal tinkle."

"I have read about you Nipper in my grandmother's diary. It is good of you to come back."

Come back ? Not to Tuesday the twentieth of June eighteen thirty-seven but back to Tuesday the seventeenth of July nineteen seventeen. My grandmother's diary, obviously it was not Queen Victoria who was speaking to Nipper, to Nipper as David and Beppo were apparently again invisible, but her grandson King George the Fifth.

"Windsor Castle," His Majesty began to explain, "was built in ten seventy during the reign of King William the First. There have been four King Williams, perhaps one day there will be a fifth such named monarch. But anyway, we are at war with Germany meaning it is inappropriate for the Royal Family to use the name Saxe-Coburg and Gotha, today I am going to change it to the House of Windsor and would be pleased Nipper if you would rechristen my grandmother's tree."

Nipper dutifully obeyed the royal decree.

Heart of oak are our ships............

On the twenty-seventh of May nineteen forty-one, which was a Friday actually, the hearts of oak within HMS Ark Royal, HMS Dorsetshire, HMS King George B and HMS Rodney sank the

German battleship Bismark. One day later the Beppo trio found themselves back in the grounds of Windsor Castle. Three of them but as was normal only Nipper was visible.

"Hello Nipper, meet my dog Susan, she's a corgi dog."

Nipper thought he could perhaps fancy her but that was not why he was there.

"I'm Elizabeth, Princess Elizabeth but people sometimes call me Lillibet. My father was in the Royal Navy you know. When I am older, I'm only fifteen, and I have a husband then a son I hope they will all serve in the Navy. Have you had a lot to drink Nipper ?"

"A fair bit," Nipper barked.

"I want you to tinkle my great-great grandmother's oak tree four times, once for HMS Ark Royal, HMS Dorsetshire, HMS King George B and once for HMS Rodney. Could you do that ?"

He could but Nipper would prefer if Corgi Susan did not watch.

"Trees are the history book of nature," King Charles the Third said. "If only they could speak what would they say ? I'd rather the Windsor Castle Oak Tree said nothing about the trump card visit from a few weeks ago ! So you three are back again; David, Beppo and Nipper you are becoming frequent visitors."

For the first time David and Beppo were not invisible.

"Queen Victoria planted this tree on the twentieth of June eighteen thirty-seven, I was born on the fourteenth of November nineteen forty-eight. Use your fingers and your paws, do the maths, I'll be eighty-four when the tree celebrates it two hundredth birthday. Not a problem, my mother made it to ninety-six and her mother to one hundred and one but Nipper if you would be so kind we'll have an early celebration.

If you're going to San Francisco
Be sure to wear some flowers in your hair

"Clowns don't wear flowers in our hair, it makes it look silly."

"Just as well we are not going to San Francisco, this is going to be just a stop off on the way to our next tree. Dogs aren't allowed on *aero*planes so Nipper will have to hide."

"Perhaps we should have had an *Aero* chocolate instead of a Yo-Yo !"

"Time to circle the world again with our Yo-Yo, the real Yo-Yo," Beppo explained, "and not another delicious mint chocolate biscuit."

"You want me to tinkle all the way up that !" Nipper barked.

"What was it King Charles said about trees being the history book of nature ?" David said. "You'd need Doctor Who to trace that thing's history."

"Indeed," Beppo confirmed. "It probably dates back further in time than when Eve served Adam his first slice of apple pie."

Adam and Eve and Pinchme all went down to bathe…
Adam and Ever were drownded who do you think was saved ?

Owch !

"I'll do the best that I can and then you can take my lead back into the yo-yo. Woof, woof !"

Job done.

"I need to comb my hair," Beppo said. "This island is so beautiful, what did you say it was called ?"

"Paradise Island," David confirmed.

Nipper found it rather hot and wanted to go for a swim in the sea.

"That sea is almost as blue as my clown's coat."

"Perhaps we could all go for a swim before we introduce Nipper to the coconut tree."

"I couldn't possibly get my clown coat wet, besides I need to find some sun cream to stop my nose getting red………"

"But it is …………"

"What's that sound, it's a bit like someone bonking on an empty oil drum."

"It's a bit calypsoish. Listen to the words."

> *Lemon tree very pretty….*
> *And the lemon flower is sweet*
> *But the fruit of the poor lemon….*
> *Is impossible to eat.*

"This isn't a lemon tree, it's a coconut tree. What tales King Charles will it be able to tell when Nipper has watered its roots ?"

"Let's find out."

"You are under arrest !"

"What ?"

"What you are doing is illegal here on Paradise Island. It makes the coconut milk taste strange. I am Officer Myers and you are all under arrest."

Beppo pushed his hands in the air and pointed to the top of the coconut tree. Responding to his action it dropped a coconut squarely and firmly on Police Officer Myer's head ! Time to play conkers.

> *Underneath the spreading chestnut tree,*
> *There we sit both you and me,*
> *Oh how happy we can be,*
> *'Neath the spreading chestnut tree.*

Time to sleep, time to prepare for the next day and next adventure. David lay his head on the pillow while Beppo curled up at the bottom of the bed. What would be tomorrow's adventure ? What would be tomorrow's chocolate ?

A Mars A Day Helps You Work Rest And Play:
(That was an advertising slogan from around fifty years ago. Today Trading Standards would never allow such. With its high sugar content a Mars a Day is not good for your health as David and Beppo are about to find out.)

"Mars is a red planet, my nose is red so I'll fit in well when we get there," Beppo said biting into his next adventure chocolate.

"Welcome to Planet Mars," an Earthman was waiting to greet the duo. "I'm Yuri."

"I'm David," David replied.

"And I'm Beppo. Yuri, that doesn't sound very English."

"Neither does Beppo," their host smiled. "I'm Russian, Yuri Gagarin."

David thought he had heard that name somewhere before.

"On the twelfth of April nineteen sixty-six I became the first man in space. My spaceship was Vostok One. "

He was still in space and now with him so were Beppo and David.

"When I flew Vostok Two I messed up, I did not set up my Sat Nav properly and ended up here on Mars. My Soviet colleagues back on Earth put out a false story saying I had been killed in a plane crash to try and cover up my stupidity."

"Didn't they want to try to rescue you ?" Beppo asked.

"From the plane crash possibly yes, but from here on Mars obviously not."

"Do you want to go home ?"

"No, I quite like it her on the Red Planet where I have a Martian girlfriend and knowing what is now happening back on the Third Planet I have no desire to return."

"What is happening ?"

"Take a bite of your chocolate and find out then use this, it is called a *smart* speaker but it is also *smart* for the eyes."

As the duo would learn *smart* in Martian translated to English means stupid !

"What's that net thing covering the Earth."

"It's called the Spiers Web, it enables all the robots to talk with one another as they trap like flies the human beings who think they rule the Earth."

"I remember being told at school," David was worried, "that Mars was the god of war. Is Mars at war with Earth."

"It is if you eat a Mars Bar," Beppo said as he took his last bite before throwing the wrapper on the ground, the red ground.

"Take that home with you," Yuri scolded. "We don't recycle here on Mars."

David looked again down the *smart whateveritwas*. "What's the thing that person has sitting on his lap ?"

"It's called a laptop. Invented here on Mars but we don't use them on the Red Planet. On your planet, formerly my planet, it helps the robots tighten the net of their spiders web."

"I think I would like to keep my nose out of that," Beppo said.

"And my lap," David added.

"He's a bit after my time," Yuri Gagarin changed the subject," but do you know who David Bowie is ?"

"Isn't he a Starman ?"

There's a Starman waitin' in the sky
He's like to come and meet us

But he thinks he's blow our minds
There's a Starman waitin' in the sky
He's told us not to blow it
'Cause he knows it's all worthwhile

"Yes, but it's his singing about where we are right now that is of interest."

Sailors
Fighting in the dance hall.
Oh man !
Look at those cavemen go.
It's the freakiest show.
Take a look at the lawman
Beating up the wrong guy.
Oh man !
Wonder if he'll ever know
He's in the best selling show.
Is there Life On Mars ?

"Is there life on Mars ?" Yuri quoted from the lyrics by way of a rhetorical question. "Of course there is, beyond we three and my girlfriend there is indeed life on Mars. Just as on any planet there are good people and there are bad people."

It's a God awful small affair
To the girl with the mousey hair,
But her mummy is yelling, No !
And her daddy has told her to go,
But her friend is nowhere to be seen.
Now she walks through her sunken dream
To the seats with the clearest view
And she's hooked to the silver screen,
But the film is sadd'ning bore
For she's lived it ten times or more.
She could spit in the eyes of fools
As they ask her to focus on

Sailors
Fighting in the dance hall.
Oh man !
Look at those cavemen go.
It's the freakiest show.
Take a look at the lawman
Beating up the wrong guy.
Oh man !
Wonder if he'll ever know
He's in the best-selling show.
Is there Life On Mars ?
It's on America's tortured brow
That Mickey Mouse has grown up a cow.
Now the workers have struck for fame
'Cause Lennon's on sale again.
See the mice in their million hordes
From Ibeza to the Norfolk Broads.
Rule Britannia is out of bounds
To my mother, my dog, and clowns,
But the film is a sadd'ning bore
'Cause I wrote it ten times or more.
It's about to be writ again
As I ask you to focus on
Sailors
Fighting in the dance hall.
Oh man !
Look at those cavemen go.
It's the freakiest show.
Take a look at the lawman
Beating up the wrong guy.
Oh man !
Wonder if he'll ever know
He's in the best-selling show.
Is there life on Mars

"There are good Martians and there are bad Martians. Take a look down the smart speaker and see what you can see this time."

Everyone, EVERYONE Beppo and David could see was walking about with a piece of plastic measuring about three inches by four inches in front of their faces. Was it possible to see anything outside these dimensions ?

"My nose wouldn't fit one of those," Beppo said thinking aloud.

"What's happening ?" David asked.

"The spiders web is controlling the flies it has caught."

"No incy wincy spider there," Beppo tried to make light of the dark situation they found themselves in.

"The God of War decreed that there is to be no fighting on the Red Planet, no Martian is allowed to be anything less than friends with his fellow Martians. What you have been watching on Earth is known as AI. On Earth A stands for *Artificial* and I for *Intelligence* but the truth is in Martian it is Alian Invasion."

"All that AI we saw down the smart speaker is happening on Earth ?"

"Look," David pointed down the smart speaker, "what are those people doing with their AI plastic things in the shops ?"

"And some of them have smaller plastic bits they are tapping on something by the tills."

"That's Artificial Intelligence *money*," Yuri clarified. "The Martian invasion destroyed money giving people tap and pay instead."

"David used money when he found me," Beppo remembered. "Four shillings and tuppence but he said it was fifty pence. What money do you use in Russia back on Earth ?"

"We use the Ruble and before you ask fifty pence is equal to zero point zero, zero, four, four pence."

"I wasn't going to ask that, I was going to ask what money the Martians use here on Mars ?"

"They use chocolate Mars Bars which they steal up the smart speaker from Earth."

"All that AI we saw down the smart speaker is really happening on Earth ?"

"You should see what AI is doing on Jupiter !"

A Mars a day helps you work, rest and play ! The two friends thought not, they'd rather have eaten a coffee cream ! Yuk ! David and Beppo, there were two of them, plural, so make that Yuk ! Yuk !

Tiger:
Can you still buy Tiger chocolate bars ? This is the author speaking. I can't find any on my local supermarket's shelf.

The Wonderful thing about Tiggers
is Tiggers are wonderful things
tops are made out of rubber
their bottoms are made out of springs
Their bouncey, trouncey, ouncey, pouncey
fun, fun, fun, fun, fun
But the most wonderful thing about Tiggers

"Did you have tigers in your circus Beppo ?"

"No animals, strictly clowns and acrobats, at least since Nellie the Elephant packed her trunk and said goodbye to the circus. Off she went with a trumpety trump Trump trump trump !"

"I wonder what a Tiger chocolate bar tastes like ? Or should that be a Tigger chocolate bar and what adventure it would give us."

"Only one way to find out."

Tyger Tyger, burning bright,
In the forests of the night;
What immortal hand or eye,
Could frame thy fearful symmetry ?

In what distant deeps or skies.
Burnt the fire of thine eyes ?
On what wings dare he aspire ?
What the hand, dare seize the fire ?

And what shoulder, and what art,
Could twist the sinews of thy heart ?
And when thy heart began to beat.
What dread hand ? And what dread feet ?

What the hammer ? What the chain,
In what furnace was thy brain ?
What the anvil ? What dread grasp.
Dare its deadly terrors clasp ?

When the stars threw down their spears
And water'd heaven with their tears:
Did he smile his work to see ?
Did he who made the Lamb make thee ?

Tyger Tyger burning bright,
In the forests of the night:
What immortal hand or eye,

Dare frame thy fearful symmetry ?

"Don't worry about my brother," Tyger said. "Walt Disney made him up to add to A A Milne's Winnie The Pooh characters of Piglet, Eeyore and Winnie himself of course. I am Tyger myself spelt T-Y-G-E-R penned by William Blake. We are actually twin brothers but not identical. Are you two related ? If you are which is the *bouncey, trouncey, ouncey, pouncey fun, fun, fun, fun, fun* one and who is the handsome one like me ?"

"This is going to be an interesting adventure," David said.

"And I think this is going to be a fun one. No red fly nets today."

"Who's coming with me to the jungle to have some *bouncey, trouncey, ouncey, pouncey fun, fun, fun, fun, fun* ?" Tigger laughed.

But before either David or Beppo could confirm their springs were ready Tyger spoke saying, "Tigers don't live in the jungle."

"Neither do tigers live in the in the forests of the night unless you spell tiger, T*y*ger and when you spell tiger Ti*gg*er you can bounce and live anywhere they like."

The jungle did sound rather more adventurous than a dark forest and neither Beppo nor David had a torch with them.

"Jump on my back and I'll bounce us off to the jungle, who knows we may even get to meet Nellie the Elephant. Nellie the Elephant packed her trunk and said goodbye to the circus. Off she went with a trumpety trump Trump trump trump !"

"I'd better join you."

"Why ?"

"Because there's a *Y* in my name and just in case you bump into an American Trumpety, Trump, Trump, Trump. Bonkers he may be but what immortal hand or eye dare frame his fearful symmetry !"

With Beppo and David riding on his back Tigger swung from jungle tree to jungle tree, each one was fun and each bouncy, trouncy, ouncey, pouncy and even five times fun.

"Have you ever seen a chocolate tree before ?"

The two were not certain if they had or not. Nipper hadn't tinkled one in an earlier adventure.

"You don't grow yo-yo's on them by any chance ?"

"I don't grow anything on them," Tigger replied, "but I do eat their fruits."

"And I eat those he drops on the ground," Tyger added.

"This is where Tiger Bars are grown."

"But it's not where you can buy elephant bars."

Who said that ?

"You can buy Golf Boxes of Chocolates, I'm Nellie by the way in case you haven't recognised me but I'd never trump them on my menu."

"Do you swing through the trees like Tigger does ?" Beppo asked.

"I weigh six and a half tons," Nellie explained, "I don't think there is a tree strong enough to hold me."

"There are the California Giant Redwoods," Tyger explained, "but they don't grow here in the jungle."

"We've been to where the California Giant Redwoods grow," David said.

"But when we went we had a dog with us not an elephant," Beppo clarified.

"What I really like is when he drops a Kit Kat from the tree, tigers are cats after all. If I can spell my Tyger name with a Y then a Kat can spell its name with a K."

"How should I spell my name," the new trumping arrival pondered ? "L E ? Doesn't work really does it ?"

"Forget trying to play the Trump card," Beppo's nose shone in the jungle, "It's only a paper tiger anyway. Stay with Nellie."

At that point five Kit Kat bars fell from a tree to the jungle floor; one for Nellie, one for Tyger, one for Tigger, one for David and one for Beppo. Time to enjoy their chocolate adventure.

The Wonderful thing about Tiggers
is Tiggers are wonderful things
tops are made out of rubber
their bottoms are made out of springs
Their bouncey, trouncey, ouncey, pouncey
fun, fun, fun, fun, fun
But the most wonderful thing about Tiggers
is I'm the only one
Tiggers are cuddily fellows
Tiggers are awfully sweet

everyone el'es is jealous
That's why I repeat and repeat
The wonderful thing about Tiggers
Is Tiggers are marvoulous chaps
They're loaded with vim and vigor
they love to leap in your laps
They're jumpy, bumpy, clumpy, thumpy
fun fun fun fun fun
But the most wonderful thing about Tiggers
Is I'm the only one
I-I-I'm the only...- oof
Ouch

KitKat:
KitKat was invented in Great Britain in the nineteen thirties and is still popular today. KitKat (KitCat ?)

What is the collective noun for a group of cats ? Is it a Kit by any chance ?

"Meow," said Macavity.

"Meow," said Skimbleshanks.

"Purrrrr," said Deuteronomy.

Macavity's a ginger cat, he's very tall and thin;
You would know him if you saw him, for his eyes are sunken in.
His brow is deeply lined with thought, his head is highly domed;
His coat is dusty from neglect, his whiskers are uncombed.
He sways his head from side to side, with movements like a snake;
And when you think he's half asleep, he's always wide awake.

You would know him if you saw him, for his eyes are sunken in………. Were Macavity's eyes sunken in ? What do sunken in eyes look like exactly ? Neither David nor Beppo recognised Macavity. He was a Kat wasn't he ?

There's a whisper down the line at 11.39
When the Night Mail's ready to depart,
Saying Skimble where is Skimble has he gone to hunt the thimble ?
We must find him or the train can't start.
All the guards and all the porters and the stationmaster's daughters
They are searching high and low,
Saying Skimble where is Skimble for unless he's very nimble
Then the Night Mail just can't go.
At 11.42 then the signal's nearly due
And the passengers are frantic to a man—
Then Skimble will appear and he'll saunter to the rear:
He's been busy in the luggage van !

David had a Horny train set at home but he and Beppo had never played together with it. David had no idea that Kats played with Hornby model railway sets.

Deuteronomy sits by the fire……….
Old Deuteronomy's lived a long time;
He's a Cat who has lived many lives in succession.
He was famous in proverb and famous in rhyme
A long while before Queen Victoria's accession
Deuteronomy sits by the fire……….

At home David and Beppo had central heating and even if there had been an open fire there was no Kat to lay down in front of it.

"Who are you and what are you doing here ?" David asked kindly.

"We are all Kats from poems written by a gentleman by the name of Old Possum," Macavity began to explain.

"We are here," Old Deuteronomy added, "to help Macavity. You have a very nice fire here to sleep by if I may say so."

"And a lovely Hornby train set for a railway cat to play with but that is not why we are here, as Deuteronomy said we are here to help Macavity."

"Who then is Macavity ? The ginger Kat ?"

Macavity's a Mystery Cat: he's called the Hidden Paw—
For he's the master criminal who can defy the Law.
He's the bafflement of Scotland Yard, the Flying Squad's despair:
For when they reach the scene of crime—Macavity's not there
!

Macavity, Macavity, there's no one like Macavity,
He's broken every human law, he breaks the law of gravity.
His powers of levitation would make a fakir stare,
And when you reach the scene of crime—Macavity's not there
!
You may seek him in the basement, you may look up in the air—
But I tell you once and once again, Macavity's not there!

Macavity's a ginger cat, he's very tall and thin;
You would know him if you saw him, for his eyes are sunken in.
His brow is deeply lined with thought, his head is highly domed;

His coat is dusty from neglect, his whiskers are uncombed.
He sways his head from side to side, with movements like a snake;
And when you think he's half asleep, he's always wide awake.

Macavity, Macavity, there's no one like Macavity,
For he's a fiend in feline shape, a monster of depravity.
You may meet him in a by-street, you may see him in the square—
But when a crime's discovered, then Macavity's not there !

He's outwardly respectable. They say he cheats at cards.
And his footprints are not found in any file of Scotland Yard's
And when the larder's looted, or the jewel-case is rifled,
Or when the milk is missing, or another Peke's been stifled,
Or the greenhouse glass is broken, and the trellis past repair
Ay, there's the wonder of the thing! Macavity's not there !

And when the Foreign Office find a Treaty's gone astray,
Or the Admiralty lose some plans and drawings by the way,
There may be a scrap of paper in the hall or on the stair—
But it's useless to investigate—Macavity's not there !
And when the loss has been disclosed, the Secret Service say:
It must have been Macavity!'—but he's a mile away.
You'll be sure to find him resting, or a-licking of his thumb;
Or engaged in doing complicated long division sums.

Macavity, Macavity, there's no one like Macavity,
There never was a Cat of such deceitfulness and suavity.
He always has an alibi, and one or two to spare:
At whatever time the deed took place—MACAVITY WASN'T THERE !
And they say that all the Cats whose wicked deeds are widely known
I might mention Mungojerrie, I might mention Griddlebone

Are nothing more than agents for the Cat who all the time
Just controls their operations: the Napoleon of Crime !

That was a somewhat lengthy explanation.

"We would like to show you a wanted poster for Macavity," Deuteronomy said softly in his old Kat voice.

"You'll have to walk with us down to the charity shop, there's no railway line going there."

"Charity shop, that's where I came from to become David's friend," Beppo explained.

He's the bafflement of Scotland Yard, the Flying Squad's despair:
For when they reach the scene of crime—Macavity's not there !

It wasn't Scotland Yard and it wasn't the Flying Squad that had put this wanted poster for Macavity in the shop window. The only crime Macavity had committed was not to be loved. The poster was from the local RSPCA animal rescue centre explaining how Macavity was needing to find his forever home.

"You gave me my forever home," Beppo said with a tear in his eye. "Could we…..?"

"I'll have to ask Mummy," David said with his fingers crossed. It was great fun having a clown live in his home, would it be great fun having a Kat as well.

"Of course he can become part of our family," Mummy said. "I'll telephone the RSPCA and make the arrangement. I'm not sure about the name Macavity, I thought he was a naughty cat. How about we call him Kit ?

Kit the Kat.

The Milky Way:

> *Hey, diddle, diddle,*
> *The cat and the fiddle,*
> *The cow jumped over the moon;*
> *The little dog laughed*
> *To see such fun,*
> *And the dish ran away with the spoon.*

"Where did that come from ?" Beppo asked. "*The cow jumped over the moon,* I assume that is where the milk came from to make the Milky Way."

"I don't like drinking milk," David explained. "Every day at school we are given one third of a pint of milk to drink before morning playtime. It's always warm and tastes yukky. Not a bit like a Milky Way chocolate bar which I really do like."

"I wonder if the dish ran away with the spoon to avoid having to drink milk while the little dog laughed because he wanted eat a Milky Way."

The little dog, that would have been Nipper. Cat ? Macavity didn't play the violin and Kit the Kat certainly does not fiddle.

> *Hey, diddle, diddle,*
> *The cat and the fiddle,*
> *The cow jumped over the moon;*
> *The little dog laughed*
> *To see such fun,*
> *And the dish ran away with the spoon.*

"Yuri Gagarin jumped over the moon, that's why he ended up on Mars. We're not going there again I hope."

"Men Very Easily Make Jugs Serving Useful Needs – Perhaps."

"What at you talking about David, it was a dish that ran away with a spoon and not a jug."

"It's something we were taught at school to remember the names of the planets in the solar system: *Men Very Easily Make Jugs Serving Useful Needs – Perhaps.* M for Mercury, V for Venus, E for Earth, M for Mars and…."

"Yeh, yeh I get it. There are hundreds of billions of planets in the Milky Way, what did they teach you at school to remember them !"

"Perhaps that's why we are here to count them and make something up."

"If we are going to do that then we'll need another Milkey Way chocolate bar each."

But on the dish there were only two chocolate bars for the spoon to serve and they weren't Milky Ways, they were Penguins.

Penguin:
People have been eating penguin biscuits since 1932 when they were invented by William McDonald, no relation to Ronald.

"So we've been to Mars and we've been to the Milky Way. I'd better dress up warm, particularly for my nose if we are now about to head to the North Pole."

"Penguins don't live at the North Pole, they live at the South Pole."

"Is it warmer there then ?"

I'm a little penguin in the snow
I slide on my tummy to and fro
I eat the fish from the deep blue sea
I'm black and white as you can see

"I don't eat fish," this strange looking little duck said. "You know what a vegetarian is, well I'm a fishiterian."

"What do you eat if you don't eat fish ?"

"Chocolate bars of course."

"Is that with or without chips ?"

"What I don't understand," Beppo puzzled, "is if you like the cold and don't eat fish then why you and your family don't live at the top of the planet and not here on its posterior."

"Polar bears live at the North Pole, I am not sure if they are fishitarians or not but they are most certainly not penguinetarians."

Fishitarians ? David had previously explained how school instilled in him a dislike of milk. Fish was served every Friday in the school dining hall with its odour penetrating the entire building for hours before dead cod in batter was served to all. Perhaps he should become a fishitarian, even perhaps go a step further and become a vegetarian.

"Polar Bears are not teddy bears," Peter, that was his name Peter the Penguin, said, "you'd not want to cuddle one of them at bedtime."

"David doesn't cuddle a teddy bear," Beppo confirmed, "I sleep at the bottom of his bed and am a witness to his nocturnal habit."

"Kit the Kat sleeps at the top of my bed," David added.

"Tell me about it, he snores !"

"No he doesn't, he purrs."

I'm a little penguin in the snow
I slide on my tummy to and fro
I do not eat the fish from the deep blue sea
I'm black and white as you can see
Another bar of chocolate
One for you and one for me

That would be nice. Beppo sent his thanks urged by two battle tanks. One had Margaret Thatcher riding in its turret and one her handbag.

"Is that the Iron Lady ?"

"No she is the Ice Lady."

And with those words this adventure came to its end. No more chocolate bars. Perhaps in time to come David and Beppo may have some fun with ice cream.

Authors note:
David aka Max here writing.

Beppo sent his thanks urged by two battle tanks.

Prime Minister Margaret Thatcher did indeed ride a battle tank in the Falkland Islands where penguins live, she did so indeed complete with her handbag when Britain won its war against Argentina.

Way back in Miss Hudson's class when Beppo performed his clown entertainment to the class Beppo appeared on stage with two toy Sherman Tanks and the words *Beppo sent his thanks urged by two battle tanks* spoken by two fellow performing string puppets.

Hello this is Beppo speaking..........
I am speaking to you dozens and dozens of years since David and I had our chocolate adventures. We are of course still very close friends, I had fun with his children and now I have fun with his grandchildren. I am still a clown, David has become a writer and scribbles away using a somewhat silly pen-name of Max Robinson. I found tucked away in a cupboard some stories my friend had written, I read them and my hair sparkled not to mention my nose glowing a bit.

If you will let me I'll now share some of those stories. So get ready for more adventures, non-chocolate but every bit as fun adventures.

Beppo

L'ESCAROT ALBERT By Max Robinson

AUTHOR'S NOTE:

(That's not me Beppo writing but Max, really David.)

When I was at school French lessons were always an excuse to be silly and mess about. French teachers were often called Frog. Now almost sixty years later, I am not proud of that fact and that my ability to speak French is confined to a maximum of five words.

Those five words I remember from my first French teacher. He invented a character Albert The Snail – l'escargot Albert who had a series of adventures which were always told to the class in French.

I have here taken my teacher's little hero and given him a series of new adventures.

Enjoy:
Je Suis L'escarot Albert:
The Cabinet Meeting:
Security Alert – Next Door's Cat:
Mickie And Minie's Party:
Woodpile Festival:
National Anthem:
Spike's Cave:
Learning To Swim:
Wiggley's Summer School:
Red Kite Airways:
L'escargot Albert Et L'escargot Alma

JE SUIS L'ESCAROT ALBERT:
Salut mesa mis, je suis l'escargot Albert. Allow me to translate that into English for you: *Hello my friends, I am Albert the snail.* I should also perhaps translate that into Amazonian but people here only speak English and I don't speak Amazonian anyway.

Yes, I am Albert the snail. These days I live in the Amazon Rain Forest, for a forest there are not all that many trees and while it does rain it does not rain a lot. I was born in France just outside a town by the name of Dunkirk. France is not a good place to live if you are a snail, the French eat snails you know and Dunkirk is not the best place to be either. For some reason people try to run away from Dunkirk and go to Britain where they do not eat snails. When Britain left the European Uninion which I am told is a democratic dictatorship I decided I too was going to wave bye-bye to France.

It was to Britain I thought I would go, I headed to the port at Dunkirk where I would stow away on a ship to England. England ? Britain ? That's a bit confusing to a little snail like me, are they the same place ? Anyway at Dunkirk I changed my mind and decided not to go to either Britain or England. I saw a big metal container with Amazon written on the side of it. Amazon, there's a rain forest there and while I am not into climbing trees, rain means the ground is wet and we snails do like the ground to be wet so Amazon it was to be. It wasn't difficult to stick myself to the metal box and soon my journey began.

So here I am mow living in a garden in a place called Milton Keynes somewhere in the Amazon Rainforest. I know I am in Amazonia as on many a day Amazon parcels are delivered to the people who live in the house. They are nice people, unlike the French they do not eat snails.

Since I moved in I have made lots of friends. There is Boris the squirrel who races round the garden like crazy, Boris the squired with his three wives and six children. Actually he only has two wives, he hasn't married number three yet. You should see the way they eat the peanuts the family put out for them, hence Boris is known as Boris The Nutter.

Richard the Robin is a talented bird. He lives behind the summer house at the bottom of the garden where he has a studio all of his own. Richard likes to paint and considers himself to be an artist but really most of his painting involve putting black dots on the backs of lady birds.

This is a bit of a music place here in Milton Amazon Keynes, there's Adam and his Ants. There are four guys who call themselves The Beetles, but insist on spelling it Beatles. Wiggly Woo, the worm who everyone looks up to as a clever man a teacher, should he perhaps give The Beatles a spelling lesson.

Queen Victoria and her boyfriend Albert are in charge of all the bees here in our not very rainy forest.

Oh I must tell you about the three pigeons who sit on the fence and look down on us all. Barry, Beatrice and Constance: B, B and C. They have appointed themselves to the job of flying all round Amazonia, finding out what is happening then sitting on the fence cooing the news to we uninterested residents. Their problem is with eyes at the sides of their heads not one of them can see what is happening right in front of their beaks. Oh well, what a shame, never mind.

I was talking about music wasn't I ? I should have told you about Vera and Lynn, two nightingales who while they do not live in our garden pop by for a visit now and then just to sing to us all. They do not live in Amazonia, they just visit, but come from somewhere they tell is called Berkeley Square.

Jeremy Crowbin. When he opens his mouth if he had a brain I tell you it would fall out. Boris The Nutter is in charge of our garden but Jeremy The Crow thinks it should be his birth right.

We have Richard the artist Robin, we all like him but there is another Richard and everything has to be hidden when he flies by. Richard Turpin the black and white magpie.

Trees, oh yes we do have trees but it is not what you would call a forest, perhaps I am wrong but we all like things the way they are, I was born in France of course, I told you that didn't I. What is French for trees ? *Des arbres*. The way to pronounce tree is French is arbour, we have an arbour but we call it the summer house. Trees or *des arbres*, birds live in them and I have so many, many friends who are birds. Not counting Richard the magpie and Jeremy Crowbin there are: sparrows, blue tits, blackbirds, thrushes and high up in the sky there are red kites. Do not believe what people tell you, birds do not eat snails. French birds may eat snails but I can assure you from my own personal experience Amazonian birds do not eat snails. You have perhaps heard about vegetarians, Amazonian birds are all snailetarians.

I have already told you about Barry, Beatrice and Constance so I'll not say any more there, not for now anyway. We do have one special little bird, her name is Jenny. Beautiful little Jenny, if I were a bird I would most certainly build a nest with her. Beautiful Jenny the Wren.

Finally there are the doves, four doves who have taken it upon themselves to bring peace and an air of calm to the garden. With Boris, his wives and crazy kids racing round like cousins of Lewis Hamilton they are important to the tranquillity here in this corner of Amazonia. I am not quite sure who Lewis Hamilton is but Barry, Beatrice and Constance report each week-end on his antics.

I have heard that not far away from Milton Keynes in Amazonia there is a place called Brazil, Brazil where the nuts grow. Perhaps we should try to persuade the Boris Family to go and live there. Without them in our garden life would be a lot more relaxed. However, even with Boris Nutter, Jeremy Crowbin and the occasional visit from Richard the thieving magpie I am very happy here and so delighted not to be living in snail-eating France.

So there you go, now you know all about me Albert The Snail. Albert and all my friends. Time for me to tell you some of our adventures. Are you sitting comfortably ? Then I'll begin.

Beppo interrupting your reading: I am sorry but I just want to check you are alright, that your face isn't aching. With David poking his tongue into the side of his mouth writing that introduction I hope it has not infected you. If you are OK then please read on.

THE CABINET MEETING:
"Albert have you heard ?"

"Heard what Wiggley Woo ?"

"Boris is asking everyone to come to a meeting this evening. Pigeons B, B and C will make an announcement later. I am going to be the secretary for the meeting so I already know about it."

"What is it all about Wiggley ?"

"I don't know, Boris will tell everyone when we get there. I know it is happening and I know I am secretary but no more. Six o'clock tonight in the summer house by the display cabinet that's where and when it's happening."

"It is going to be a cabinet meeting then. If it is to discuss a nut shortage then I am not worried but could be Boris is going to announce that he and his family are moving to live in Brazil."

B, B and C duly announced the forthcoming cabinet meeting but said nothing about its purpose and never once mentioned nuts. "We will bring you a report the moment the cabinet meeting is over," Barry, Beatrice and Constance cooed from their place sitting on top of the fence.

"Well, we are not going," Adam said, "me and my ants have a new song to rehearse ahead of the festival."

"That's not for weeks yet," Beatle John observed.

"I will be going no matter what it is about, I need to be there in order to object," Jeremy Crowbin squawked.

"Please come Albert," Wiggley Woo pleaded. "As Cabinet Secretary your support would be very much appreciated. I am nervous."

"Worms should not be nervous," Jeremy announced. "Worms should be decisive."

"A bit like you are you mean Crowbin."

"I object to that !"

"Sorry we won't be able to make it," the Red Kites spread their wings.

"We will bring you a news report once the cabinet meeting is over, " B, B and C explained.

"Thanks but no thanks, no need. We are Red Kites, so we watch Sky because that's where we fly."

"As you wish."

"I object to that," Jeremy crowed.

"Now we are no longer part of the democratic dictatorship of The European Disunity," Boris began, "we need to consider our border control and immigration policies. How are we going to police the garden fence ?"

"I do not agree," said Jeremy Crowbin.

Everyone sighed.

"What do you not agree with ?"

"I am not sure yet."

"Can you please make a note of that Cabinet Secretary."

Wiggley Woo duly wrote something down on his hermaphrodite pad.

"There is more," Boris continued. "Amazon yesterday delivered a big parcel to the family in the house."

"What did it contain ? This parcel from Amazon ?"

"Everything needed to build a garden pond."

"That will be nice," Robin said. "I could paint a picture of it."

"With a pond there will be fish. Immigrants."

Boris shrugged his squirrel shoulders. "I do not know, there were no fish in the Amazon parcel. We are going to have to protect our fishing rights, we cannot have members of the European Disunion interfering in the waters of our pond."

As a snail I tend to move slowly but with the news of a pond in the garden my mind was racing ahead of Nutter Boris. "Where there is a pond there will be frogs."

"Frogs !" Crowbin exclaimed. "Frogs are French. I object."

"I used to be French," I began explaining. "Not only do the French eat snails they also eat frogs !"

"Exactly," Boris gave a squirrel smile. "I propose we offer political asylum to any frog who wants to live in our pond."

"Won't the fish object ?"

"The fish and the frogs will need to live in harmony and we must welcome them into our community."

"Yes Boris, we must. We must also ban all French fishermen from our waters."

"What about China ?" Jenny Wren said. "In China they make soup out of birds nests, we cannot allow any Chinese people across our borders.

There was a huge cheer from all birds in attendance. "We must protect our nests at all costs. We cannot allow a single Chinaman into the garden."

Jeremy Crowbin wanted to say something but even his loud voice could not be heard above the birdsong of our sparrows, blackbirds, thrushes, blue tits and more.

"May I propose," I said, "that we ask our Cabinet Secretary to put up noticed all the way around the garden fence declaring it to be our sovereign border, welcoming all frogs from France and banning all nest-eating Chinese."

There was a strong murmur of agreement.

"We have a proposal from Snail Albert," Boris said, "do we have someone to second the motion ?"

"I will do that," Richard the Robin said, "and I will paint the notices to put on the fence."

In due course the pond was installed in our little corner of Amazonia Milton Keynes. Two fish came to live in our sovereign waters, two new friends Koi and Carp. They kept themselves very much to themselves but from the waters they would look up and smile. Bees Victoria and Albert instructed all of their hive to sting any European Disunity member who disrespected our fishing rights.

Two frogs, Barney and Mrs Barney escaped the culinary eccentricities of France to live in our community. They and our fish Koi and Carp got on very well becoming good friends. Mr and Mrs Barney promised to add some tadpoles to the pond.

Richard Robin did produce his border control notices and our red kites flew far and wide telling all they needed a full passport and visa if they wanted to come anywhere near us. As clever as Wiggley Woo is he did not know how to spell the words passport and visa, at least that is what he said, so our border was secure.

Nutter Boris decided a weekly cabinet meeting was a good idea. We all agreed save for Jeremy Crowbin who objected but was always in attendance. Wiggley Woo was a very good cabinet secretary and kept meticulous records of all came up for debate. B. B and C gave their reports but most of us waited for the red kites to come back with news from the sky.

Subjects for discussion included how many black spots Richard should be allowed to paint on the back of a ladybird to the length of prison sentence should be given to Magpie Turpin if ever he could be apprehended. Then came the special meeting called to discuss next door's cat.

SECURITY ALERT – NEXT DOOR'S CAT:

"It's a Siamese Cat," everyone was saying. "Siam is in China and in China they make soup out of birds nest."

"Mr Cabinet Secretary, Wiggley Woo will you please record that Siam is not in China," Squirrel Boris instructed. Then aside he said. "Siam is as close to China as Milton Keynes is to the Amazon Rain Forest."

What did he mean by that ? Who was he speaking to ? Probably Jeremy Crowbin.

"We have received political asylum requests," Wiggley said, "from Spike a hedgehog who lives in next door's garden and from mice Mickey and Minnie."

"I assume there are no objections to their applications. Jeremy ?"

"I don't object but I do object to your asking me !"

I decided to speak. "I do not think that a Chinese cat is going to respect our borders."

"Is China in the Democratic Dictatorship of The European Disunion ?" Richard Robin asked, "I do not know how to paint in Chinese."

Nutter Boris tried to be patient. He drew breath. "Siam is NOT in China and China is NOT in The European Disunion."

I spoke again. "Just because we give asylum to mice and a hedgehog does not stop a cat from Siam or anywhere else climbing over our fence. Cats eat mice and cats eat birds as well."

"I object to that," Jeremy Crowbin said. "I object to cats eating birds."

For once we all agreed with Jeremy but then he was a bird.

"Do cats eat snails ?"

"If they come from China they probably do. Have toasted snail as a side dich to their birds nest soup."

This was turning into a complex cabinet meeting. Wiggly Woo was having a hard job keeping up with everything. Even B, B and C were having difficulty trying to write their news report. They had to be able to coo it out once the meeting had finished, they could not allow the red kites to broadcast it from Sky.

"What about Jake ?" Mrs Boris, or should I say Boris's girlfriend Miss Boris, did not usually say anything at meetings but would smile and look pretty.

We all knew who Jake was. Jake the dog, Jake the dog there's no one quite like Jake the dog. He lived in the house with the family but visited the garden several times a day to do what dogs do in the garden. He would bark, particularly bark at Boris and the BBC but he never barked at me. We all knew his bark was worse than his bite. In all probability he had never bitten anyone in his entire doggie life.

"Jake," Boris pondered aloud. "Yes, that may work but whenever he sees me in the garden he chases me."

"He's never caught you ?"

"No, his bark is worse than his bite but I would rather not check his bite out." Boris paused to ponder again. "Perhaps we could offer him the post of head of border security."

I liked the idea.

"We could also put him in charge of chasing off thieving Richard Turpin."

"I object, Jake barks at me."

"If we could all bark Jeremy we would all bark at Crowbin."

"We need someone to speak with Jake, any volunteers ?"

Cabinet Secretary Wiggley Woo waited to record the name of the one who Boris was inviting to volunteer. B, B and C were eager to know who they had to include in their news report. It was of little consequence, dogs never much pay attention to the news.

"What about you John, Paul, George, Ringo ?"

"No, there never was a dog in Strawberry Fields nor in Sergeant Pepper's band which was too lonely for dogs. What about you Adam ?"

"It's not really something ants would be into."

"I'll do it." Whatever made me say that ? "What about you doves," I added. "Peace is your thing."

"We are very busy preparing for the festival."

Festival ? What was all this talk about a festival ?

"I will be there," Victoria said. "After all I am the monarch and head of state."

Boris looked at our Queen Bee, it appeared from his nutty expression that he thought he was in charge.

"As Cabinet Secretary I will be there as well," Wiggley Woo added. "So it will be Her Majesty Queen Victoria, Ambassador Albert and myself as Cabinet Secretary who meet with Doggie Jake,"

Doggie Jake was very friendly. "Of course I will police the fence, I have already chased the cat away a few times but now I give you my word it will never enter our garden again. You know it's a Chinese cat don't you ?"

"Siamese yes, but somebody told me Siam is not in China."

"Its name is Meowsetongue and that is Chinese," Jake barked. "Besides, it uses a smart phone and a Chinese Huawei at that !"

"Bombinate," Queen Victoria said. "Bombinate is the sound bees make when they are working, buzzing around. It can block phone signals so Meowsetongue will not be able to use his Chinese Huawei phone along our borders."

I was curious. "Is China in the European Disunion ?"

It was Wiggley Woo, well after all he is the clever one, who spoke. "China is an even bigger democratic dictatorship than the European Disunion but thankfully it is far too far away to be a part."

"Is it anywhere near Brazil where the nuts come from ?" I asked but Wiggley did not reply.

And so it was that Mickey and Minnie Mouse together with Spike The Hedgehog were granted political asylum and came to live in our garden. Jake was as good as his word Keeping China's Siamese cat Meowsetongue away from our border.

Beppo interrupting again. David my friend this tale you are telling, if you will forgive me from saying so, is silly. No clowns, I am a clown if you have not noticed, are meant to be silly but what you are saying here is silly to the point of being sensible.

MICKIE AND MINIE'S PARTY:

With the treat from Meowsetongue and the rest of the European Disorder retreating ours was a happy garden. Boris continued to race around like Lewis Hamilton's cousin, whoever Lewis Hamilton is, but Victoria was our head of state, Victoria was our queen.

Spikey The Hedgehog together with Mickey and Minnie were welcomed into our garden soon becoming valued members of the community.

I was once a foreign immigrant but now I am a Gardonian and proud to be a loyal subject of Queen Bee Victoria.

When Mickey and Minnie said they were going to throw a party everyone was very excited, very excited indeed. Everyone in Gardonia was invited including Jeremy Crowbin who for once did not object.

Doggie Jake was to be guest of honour. B, B and C made sure the party was headline news while the Red Kites gave the news to Sky.

"My wife is a good cook," Mickey said, "so do not eat anything before you come to the party. As for me, I am a bit of a musician so I will organise the after dinner entertainment."

"What instrument do you play ?" Beatle George asked.

"The Mouseorgan."

"Name a song you play, something about a mouse."

"A mouse lives in a windmill in Old Amsterdam."

"You cannot play that ! Boris said sternly. "Amsterdam is in the European Disunion."

"How about hickory, dickory dock a mouse ran up the clock ?"

"Definitely," Beatle George said. "I'll dance to that."

"Let me change the subject," Squirrel Boris spoke again. "Will nuts be on the menu ?"

"Certainty," Minnie gave a mousey smile. "I do a very special nut roast."

"What kind of nuts ?"

"Brazil nuts."

"I have ordered them on Amazon," Doggie Jake explained, "Minnie can cook them for the party."

So Brazil is not in the European Disunion. Is it part of Amazonia Milton Keynes.

The nutroast was delicious, even Jeremy Crowbin said it was. Koi and Carp enjoyed the crumbs we threw into the pond. "It was a gastronomic delight," Wiggley Woo said. That's a nice word – gastronomic, well Wiggley is the clever one here in Gardonia.

"Time for the entertainment," Mickey said. "I have my mouseorgan here and ready. Time to dance."

Jake was as excited as a dog with two tails. Boris was as excited as a squirrel with three tails.

We danced the conga then Mickey's mouseorgan gave us a dance competition.

"When Amazon delivered the nuts," Jake explained, "they also delivered a box of pineapples."

"So all gather round the trees and start pushing," Mickey grinned through his mouseorgan as he played Agadoo. Spikey the Hedgehog won that dance.

Wiggley Woo won the twist, that's what worms do isn't it – twist. Adam and his ants danced the limbo better than any of us so were declared the winners. I came last ! Well how was I meant to get my shell under the limbo stick ? I also was useless at hokey cokey, I do not have any legs left or right to put in and out ! It was difficult to pick a winner for the birdie dance but in the end after dancing it five times the speckled thrushes won the prize. Throughout Boris danced like a centipede with three legs, he didn't win anything.

What a wonderful place Gardonia is. As the party came towards its end Bee Albert buzzed: "Attention everyone, my wife would like to speak."

"Thank you Mickie and thank you Minnie for such a lovely party. I would like to thank my fellow bees for blocking phone waves from China penetrating our garden but I have a special way to thank Doggie Jake for keeping everyone safe from Mouseytongue and all who would threaten our happiness. Step forward Jake."

Jake did as he was told.

"Kneel down Jake."

What was happening ? We all wondered what was happening.

"Arise Sir Jake, Knight of Gardonia."

Jake was as happy, Jake was as proud as a dog with two hundred and twenty-two tails. Jake the Dog, there's no one quite like Jake the Dog.

Wiggley carefully wrote everything down for the cabinet records while B, B and C broadcast a news report which no one listened to, no one listened because we were all there anyway.

WOODPILE FESTIVAL:
It was not usual for the doves to attend a cabinet meeting and when on the odd occasion they did come along nobody from their community ever spoke but this day was different.

"The Festival," one said, "is not a matter for governmental discussion."

"I disagree," Jeremy Crowbin said. "I agree to disagree."

Squirrel Boris was unusually quiet and lost for words. Not so the doves. "Cabinet Secretary Wiggley Woo will you please ensure from now on that at any time you record the word Festival it is done so with a capital F."

Boris had something to say, how else could he claim to be the Prime Nutter of Gardonia ? "Cabinet Secretary that has my approval, from now on will you also record the words european and disunion in small case letters. Thank you."

"I agree to disagree."

"Thank you Jeremy."

The doves took back control of the meeting. "This is to be at three day festival of music," they all spoke together. "Three days of peace and love, the peace and love we all enjoy here in Gardonia."

"How many do you expect to come to the Festival ?" It was B, the first B in B, B and C who asked ?

"How far do you want us to announce the Festival ?" B, the second B in B, B and C then asked ?

C, as in B, B and C had to say something but could not think of anything to say. Usually when B, B and C had no news to report they just made it up but before fake news could fall out of C's beak the Red Kites said. "You can count on us to put all the news out on Sky."

Repeating his question B number one asked, "How many people do you expect to come to the festival ?"

Speaking together the doves did not answer but volunteered some different information. "We are going to make the stage out of the wood in the corner at the bottom of the garden, the woodpile."

"You mean that stock of wood nobody uses any longer ?"

"Woodstock, woodpile and yes nobody uses it so it is just sitting there. It will make a perfect stage for people to perform on."

"We will be there of course," The Beatles said.

Wiggley Woo was not sure if he should write that down as Beatles or Beetles. In the end he decided to use both versions, both using capital letters.

"So will be the Ants and me," Adam confirmed.

"I have a song," Nightingale Vera chirped.

"And I will play my mouseorgan again."

"Indeed you will," Minnie smiled, "and I will cook up some nutroast for our guests."

"How many guests will there be ?"

"I can sing Doggie In The Window," Jake wagged his tail. Both of them. (Both tails plural.)

"Better make that Sir Doggie in the window Sir Jake."

"How many people are coming ?" Was that question ever going to be answered ?

"We have two special guest artists for our woodpile stage, two butterflies Daniel and Gerrard."

"Gerrard, that sound a bit european disunion !"

"Not any more, they live in Amazonia now and want to come and live with us all in Gardonia."

"But how many people are you expecting to come to our Woodpile Festival ?"

"As many as want to come to and listen to the music, as many as want to come to Gardonia, as many as want to come in love and peace." An answer but not an answer to B, B and C's question.

I was listening very carefully, what could I do at Woodpile ? I volunteered to help Minnie with her nutroast. Spike the Hedgehog said he would also help.

There were three doves at the cabinet meeting, three doves but nobody knew their names. "I need to record your names," Wiggley Woo said. "Would you be so kind as to tell me so I can worm-write them down."

"I am Jimmy and this is Hen, she's a lady dove."

"And I am Rick."

"Jimmy-Hen-Rick. Thank you."

The answer to the frequently asked question was actually thirty thousand. Gardonia is, as a little snail like me thinks, a very big area and a little too big for me to count as far as thirty-thousand. I assumed the doves Jimmy, Hen and Rick could count that far.

Caterpillars, butterflies, birds of all kinds, frogs, hedgehogs, ladybirds, earwigs, buzzy bees. Would there be any snails ? I would like that, it would be good to stop being the only snail in Gardonia.

Changing the subject, how many ingredients would Amazon have to deliver for Minnie to make enough nutroast to feel thirty thousand ? I rather guess that depends on how many nutter squirrels turn up.

"I am going to make some hedgehog cakes," Spikey said. "You will like my hedgehog cakes I promise you."

I knew I would.

What could I make to feed thirty-thousand people at our Woodpile Festival ? I could not think of anything at all. I could not think of anything I could make for our visitors to eat, nothing at all.

"Then how about something for people to drink ?" Sir Jake suggested.

"What a good idea, no wonder Queen Victoria made you a Knight of The Garden."

"Forget the Sir stuff, I am just Jake. Jake the Dog."

"And there's no one quite like Jake the Dog," I said then added, "What do you suggest I could make to drink ?"

"Amazon."

"What ?"

"Amazon, I am going to order some coconuts."

"Who for ? Boris ?"

"No, not for Boris but we'll let him pay the bill."

"I have never heard of coconuts, do they come from Brazil ?

"No they come from Amazon and you can make a great drink

from them ?"

"Coconut Cola ?"

"Yeh, Coco Cola."

I beamed a great big snail smile.

Coco Cola specially brewed for you by Albert The Snail to drink at Woodpile Festival. I would ask Richard Robin the artist to make a display sign.

The stage at Woodpile Festival was due to commence playing at midday on Saturday, by half past nine there were sixty-two people waiting for its music. By eleven there were ten times the anticipated. I can not count that far but B, B & C even though they have difficulties seeing far beyond their own beaks assured the numbers were correct. The Red Kites on Sky said even more people were on their way. Prince Albert buzzed himself round welcoming everyone to his wife's realm. By the time Mickey lifted his mouseorgan we were half a million strong.

Jake was constantly ordering, re-ordering and ordering more supplies from Amazon as half a million friends were drinking Snail Albert's Coco Cola faster than I could brew it. Prince Albert organised a team of buzzy bees to help both myself and Mini Mouse with her nut roast.

Richard Robin was painting picture after picture to record all that was happening on stage and views of all looking on. Then the other Richard, Magpie Rickard Turpin, appeared sitting on the fence. Immediately Jake changed from Amazon mode to his security mode. His bark took on the fierce threat of a bite.

"I am here to apologise," Magpie Turpin said. "Your music is reforming me. Please may I sit here and listen ?"

Squirrel Boris had been uncharacteristically quiet during the festival but just as he was about to sink his fifteenth pint of Coconut Cola he added his opinion.

Jeremy Crowbin who had only had two glasses as he objected to Coco Cola added his objection to what was happening.

"Please Magpie Robin ?" Said. This music is beautiful. Please."

"Let him stay," Prince Albert said, "there is a greater situation and danger on the other side of the realm."

I realised only then that Prince Albert, husband of Queen Bee Victoria, and Yours Truly have the same name. Albert The Snail and Albert The Royal Buzzy Bee. Anyway…

Albert had already ordered two hundred bees to surround Mousetongue. On his order they would all sting.

"Chinese cats are not welcome at Woodpile," Boris ordered.

Joining the gathering Jimmy, Hen and Rich spoke. "At Woodpile everyone is welcome, even nutty self-important squirrels, everyone is welcome at Woodpile providing they are here in peace and in love."

"I do not come from China, I am from Siam. I am a Siamese Cat."

"Same difference," Boris gave a display of his geographical ignorance. "Siam, China, it's all part of the european disunion."

B, B and C were soon on the scene trying hard to see what was happening beyond the end of their beaks. Overhead the Red Kites were reporting for Sky.

Jake growled.

"Please there is no need to growl," Mouseytongue said. "I am really a pussycat."

"A Chinese pussycat with a Huawei smart phone."

"It's broken."

"Broken," Jeremy Crowbin said. "That's good but I object."

"I don't object," Mouseytongue said. "I don't want a smart phone, I just want to listen to the music. I am, a pussycat. Honestly. I will even become a vegetarian pussycat and eat only nut roast if you will let me stay and listen to the music."

"Can I interest you in a glass of Coco Cola ?" I asked.

"Pour me another while you are at it," Nutter Boris said in confirmation that Mouseytongue was allowed to stay and listen to music at Woodpile.

"We need to go," Jimmy, Hen and Rich explained. "We are on stage in just a few minutes."

"I need to go as well," Prince Albert added, "my wife is waiting for me. "We are going to watch Jimmy, Hen and Rich, we have been told their performance will be something very special."

"I do promise to be a good pussycat," Mouseytongue confirmed, "honestly I do."

Prince Albert thought he was probably telling the truth but just in case three hundred bee stings remained at the ready.

"I object," Jeremy Crowbin said.

"Could I have another pint of Coconut Cola ?" Boris asked.

"This will be last orders," I explained. "I am closing the bar while Jimmy, Hen and Rich are on stage. I want to listen to them."

Even if the bar had remained open when Jimmy, Hen and Rich started to coo on stage nobody would have wanted a drink. Everyone stopped eating. Richard Robin stopped painting for the first time during the festival. From Blackbirds to Jake The Dog, from Cabinet Secretary Wiggley Woo to Hedgehog Spike we all wanted to give our full attention to this performance. Jeremy stopped crowbin, B, B and C stopped trying to look beyond the end of their beaks and turned up the volume to their ears, the Red Kites floated in the air as they looked down.

On the wings of a snow white dove
We bring you our peace and love
A sign from above
On the wings of a dove

When trouble surrounds us
When sadness comes
The body grows weak
The spirit grows numb
When these things beset us
Please do not forger
Our peace and our love
On the wings of a dove

On the wings of a snow white dove
We bring you our peace and love
A sign from above
On the wings of a dove

The moment Jimmy, Hen and Rich stopped cooing half a million guests in the audience started to cheer and applause. With a snail having no hands to clap together I cheered, I cheered very loudly. Then everyone fell silent as Queen Victoria buzzed up into the air.

"My husband and I would like to invite Jimmy, Hen and Rich to sing that song again. I wish to tell you all that we are amused, we are very amused indeed. Thank you, Jimmy, Hen and Rich."

On the wings of a snow white dove
We bring you our peace and love
A sign from above
On the wings of a dove

When trouble surrounds us
When sadness comes
The body grows weak
The spirit grows numb
When these things beset us
Please do not forger
Our peace and our love
On the wings of a dove

On the wings of a snow white dove
We bring you our peace and love
A sign from above
On the wings of a dove

Again after the song the applause erupted, this time silenced as Prince Albert buzzed.

"My wife and I would like to invite Jimmy, Hen and Rich to sing that song again."

On the wings of a snow white dove
We bring you our peace and love
A sign from above
On the wings of a dove

When trouble surrounds us
When sadness comes
The body grows weak
The spirit grows numb
When these things beset us
Please do not forger
Our peace and our love
On the wings of a dove

On the wings of a snow white dove
We bring you our peace and love
A sign from above
On the wings of a dove

By Royal Command Woodpile Festival ended with every artist standing on stage together. There were The Beatles, Adam And His Ants, Nightingale Vera, Mickey and his mouseorgan, Butterflies Daniel and Gerrard, all gathered round Jimmy, Hen and Rich to sing once again On The Wings Of A Dove.

On the wings of a snow white dove
We bring you our peace and love
A sign from above
On the wings of a dove

When trouble surrounds us
When sadness comes
The body grows weak
The spirit grows numb
When these things beset us
Please do not forger
Our peace and our love
On the wings of a dove

On the wings of a snow white dove
We bring you our peace and love
A sign from above
On the wings of a dove

"Nutter Boris," Prince Albert said. "When everyone has left my wife commands you to call a cabinet meeting in the summer house."

Squirrel Boris nutted his head towards Wiggley Woo.

"I will make that happen Your Royal Highness." The Cabinet Secretary stood to attention.

Beppo what a silly clown I have been ! Clown are silly of course, that's what fun is all about. Naivety is not a word to be found the Oxford Clown Dictionary of English but that is what I have been. You'll probably need to be as old as David to realise the events, both from recent and from not so recent history my friend has been giving his tongue to tickle his cheek. Cheek ? Cheeky David !

NATIONAL ANTHEM:
"Prime Nutter," Queen Bee Victoria began, "this will not be a long meeting."

"Your Majesty."

Cabinet Wiggley Woo was poised to write.

"Gardonia's Woodpile Festival will go down in history, it is already a legend." She paused then said, "Gardonia is a legend it its own time."

How fortunate I came to live here, how fortunate I left France.

Her Majesty continued addressing the cabinet meeting. "We need an anthem, we need a national anthem. Prince Albert and I have talked about this many times. Now Jimmy, Hen and Rich have given us a beautiful piece which I am here commanding will become Gardonia's National Anthem."

"Should we sing it now Your Majesty ?"

"Indeed we should Prime Nutter."

On the wings of a snow white dove
We bring you our peace and love
A sign from above
On the wings of a dove

When trouble surrounds us
When sadness comes
The body grows weak
The spirit grows numb
When these things beset us
Please do not forger
Our peace and our love
On the wings of a dove

On the wings of a snow white dove
We bring you our peace and love
A sign from above
On the wings of a dove

SPIKE'S CAVE:

Spike was the kind of person who tended to keep himself a bit to himself. I say *was* in the past tense, that has changed. Let me tell you how the change came about.

"Have you ever heard of Amazon Spike, Spike ?" Jake asked.

"No Sir Jake, I have not."

"Forget the Sir stuff, have you ever heard of Amazon Spike, Spike ?"

"No, I can't say I have, what's it all about ? Nails, swords, needles ? They are spikes aren't they ?"

"Different kinds of spikes. Amazon Spike is a membership thing meaning you get free and faster deliveries."

"Since Woodpile Festival more people have come to live here in Gardonia."

"It's great isn't it, I am one of those lucky new residents." Mousetongue came to join the conversation.

"I have an idea," Jake continued. "If we were to buy lots of stuff on Amazon Spike we could set up a little shop where residents could buy bits and pieces for themselves."

"Sounds a good idea," Spike liked Jake's thinking.

"Would you run a little shop to sell it ? You could call it Spike's Cave."

Spike thought for a moment, a short moment before happily agreeing.

"There's a place next to the Woodpile stage which would be prefect."

"Could I help ?" Mousetongue asked. "I would like to if you would let me."

"Of course."

"There's a tree log there, I could sit on it and be your Catalog."

As I overheard the conversation I gave a snail smile.

"Just one thing," Mouseytongue said. "I do not like the name Mousetongue, do you think I could change it ?"

"I am not sure," Jake give it some thought. "We may have to ask Queen Bee Victoria for royal ascent."

"I will ask her," Prime Nutter Boris joined our little group. "What would you like for a new name ?"

"I have been thinking about Samuel, Sammy," our new feline resident said.

"I will ask Her Majesty."

"I was also wondering if Richard Robin could repaint me, perhaps changing my Siamese look to something more black and white."

"Excellent idea !" Boris nutted. "At the same time he could give me a makeover and paint the fur on the top of my head yellow."

Queen Victoria gave her Royal Ascent to the change of name and for a new black and white look for Sammy. As for Boris having a yellow head she said that was a paintbrush too far !

Over the next week Jake, Sammy and Spike worked like crazy to stock Spike's Cave with all kinds of fun bits and pieces ahead of it opening. Richard painted a Grand Opening poster which Sammy put up on the catolog,

B, B and C refused to announce the opening as they claimed they did not do advertising. The Red Kites did not have a problem with this so put it out every hour on Sky.

The opening was a great success. I had brewed a few gallons of Coconut Cola for Spike to sell. Mini added two giant boxes of her famous nut roast. Jeremy Crowbin donated some feathers to be made into quill pens. Adam made a special recording of Ant Music which he released on GCD – Gardonia Compact Disc. John, Paul, George and Ringo bottled Beatlejuice which was very popular. Beatlejuice ? Perhaps I had a rival for my Coconut Cola.

Spike's Cave was very popular and at the heart of our community, a community which had increased since Woodpile and as more people found the sense to leave the european disunion Gardonia, Milton Keynes, Amazonia would continue to grow. How proud I was to be a part of the community. How lucky I was to have found that Amazon container at Dunkirk.

Dunkirk, that was a long time ago. Actually in the lifetime of a snail it is not a long time but for me it was a very happy time that began as soon as I set sail for Amazonia. Amazonian Rain Forest, well it does rain a bit here and after all snails like the rain as it helps us slide along the ground. I am the only snail here so perhaps I need to change the plural into singular. There are two Red Kites, four Beatles, two Mice Mickey and Minnie, three news reporters B, B and C, three white doves Jimmy, Hen Rich, in the pond there are Koi and Carp. So many ants, so many ladybirds, so many buzzy bees but only one snail, me.

LEARNING TO SWIM:
The pond had developed into a special but secretive place. The flowers around its banks and the lilies which floated in its surface were full of colour. Koi and Carp lived there and while they would look up and smile at we all they could not get out of the water to join us. Barney and Mrs Barney lived on the pond

for part of each day and for the other bit they roamed around the garden.

"My wife and I are amphibians," Barney explained.

"What is an amphibian ?"

"If you want a dictionary definition then Wiggley Woo is your man but very simply you are an amphibian, I am an amphibian and my wife is an amphibian. We live partly in the pond and partly on the ground. You could do the same."

"I couldn't."

"Snails can live in water if it takes their fancy."

"That is true Albert," Mrs Barney confirmed. "We originate from France, Monsieur Barney, moi et vous Albert, nous sommes Tous Francais."

I struggled with the translation into English. I am English, I do not need to parler French.

"English snails swim."

"I do not swim, I am English and I am a snail."

"Then perhaps it is time you learned to swim mon amie Albert."

"Are you going to teach me then my friend Barney ?"

Koi and Carp are better qualified.

The water was cold, if this was what it meant to be an amphibian then take it away and I will live on firm ground. Perhaps swimming would be better for Boris.

"I object to swimming," Jeremy explained, "It is not something for a Crowbin."

"I am afraid I am too busy being the catalog and helping out in Spike's Cave."

"There are water Beatles," Paul said, "perhaps my mates and I will have a go later. Much later."

"I am more at home in Berkeley Square," Nightingale Vera excused herself from the swimming lesson. "I never did take to the water splashing against the white cliffs of Dover."

"Let me know how you get on, after all what is an eel other then a worm in water ? I can't join you today, I've got loads of cabinet writing to do."

"Thank you for your support Wiggley Woo."

Water, water everywhere and not a drop that was warm.

"Move around and you will soon feel warm," Koi said.

"How am I supposed to move around in liquid ?"

"Snails crawl," Carp explained. "Swim the crawl."

I entered the water with apprehension and feeling trepidation, they are big words for a snail to use. I entered the water feeling silly and not knowing what I was about to do. I left the water feeling cold and wet, having managed to crawl a few strokes I still felt silly. If I really knew what apprehension and trepidation meant I could tell you if I still felt them or not. If it were not for one thing I would not venture into the water again.

Actually that is not quite correct, if it were not for two things I would never go there again. Those two things are Koi and Carp who until I ventured into their pond were strangers and now they are friends, good friends. A stranger is only a friend you have yet to meet.

The next time I went for a crawl in the pond the Water Beatles joined me. They kept singing a song about a yellow submarine. Wiggley pretended he was an eel, he was rather good at pretending. Jeremy pretended he was an ugly duckling but objected so returned to being a Crowbin. Boris objected saying it was not his style but made all of his wives, girlfriends and children swim.

"Dogs can swim," Barney said, "it is born into their nature."

"Not into mine it is not, Besides, I've got another Amazon order to place."

"And I am busy with the catalog," Samuel gave a pussycat grin.

Daniel and Gerard danced from lily pad to lily pad.

And so it was a swimming pool was added to the realm of Gardonia here in Milton Keynes, Amazonia. What next ?

WIGGLEY'S SUMMER SCHOOL:
I did not think it was a good idea but the idea was my friend Wiggley Woo's so I did not say anything. Not that I ever say that much in cabinet meetings anyway.

"Which school did you go to Prime Nutter Boris ?" Wiggley asked.

"It was a harrowing experience that I can tell you."

"You went to Harrow ?"

"No, my school was a bit of a mess. Eton Mess, always served when we played cricket at Harrow. Double helpings when we won. Eton Mess, yummy !"

"What is Eaton Mess ? Was that how tidy you kept your desk ?"

"Eton Mess is ice cream, meringue, fruit and fresh cream. Mini Mouse you should make some and Spike you and Samuel could sell it in your cave."

Sometimes in cabinet meetings Boris scampered round subjects like he scampered round outside. Wiggley brought everything back on track.

"I will teach The Beetles how to spell, Richard can teach people to paint and Albert can teach people to speak French."

"I do not speak French," I quickly corrected my friend.

"Quite right," Boris said. "France is in the european disunion and besides there are only two languages in this world: English and foreign. Cabinet secretary please make sure you use a small *f* for foreign."

Life was getting really busy. One afternoon swimming every week, two and sometimes three visits a day to Spike's Cave, how was I going to fit in a lesson at Summer School if the cabinet passed it ? On top of all that I was still brewing Coco Cola.

Albert, the other Albert – Prince Albert entered the room. We all stood up and sang our National Anthem.

On the wings of a snow white dove
We bring you our peace and love
A sign from above
On the wings of a dove

When trouble surrounds us
When sadness comes
The body grows weak
The spirit grows numb
When these things beset us
Please do not forger
Our peace and our love
On the wings of a dove

On the wings of a snow white dove
We bring you our peace and love
A sign from above
On the wings of a dove

"I think we should put science on the curriculum ?"

"Science, " Samuel said. "What do we need science for. My smart phone broke, I threw it away and now I can live happily without it. Without science."

We all wanted to agree with Samuel but was it right to agree with something against a member of our Royal Family. For once Jeremy spoke for us all.

"I disagree," he said.

His Royal Highness thought then said, "We live in a democracy so Mr Cabinet Secretary I withdraw my suggestion."

What could I learn at Wiggley's Summer School ? What lesson could I take ? What subject could I teach ?

Ballroom dancing ? I don't think so.

House building ? After all I do carry my own home on my back everywhere I go.

I would like to learn to play the guitar like The Beatles do. Or should that be like The Beetles do. The problem is I do not have any fingers to pluck the strings.

There was going to be an opera class, Daniel and Gerard were planning to sing something from Madame Butterfly by someone called Puccini, whoever he is. Boris, however, insisted it would have to be called Mrs Butterfly. Someone said there was a part for a snail in Mozart 's Music Flute so I decided to give it a try.

Neither happened. Boris was sceptical because Mr Mozart and Mr Puccini, although it was not around in their day, originated from the european disunion. "I would prefer something British," he said.

Is Britain in Amazonia ? Why couldn't we have geography lessons in Wiggley's Summer School ?

"Cats !" Samuel declared excitedly. "Cats by Andrew Lloyd Webber ! Bags I sing Skimbleshanks."

"Who is Skimbleshanks ?"

"Skimbleshanks The Railway Cat, the cat of the railway train," Sammy started to sing.

Skimbleshanks the Railway Cat, the Cat of the Railway Train
There's a whisper down the line at eleven thirty-nine
When the Night Mail's ready to depart
Saying, Skimble, where is Skimble ?
Has he gone to hunt the thimble ?
We must find him or the train can't start

"I will be Macavity," Nutter Boris insisted.

Macavity's a mystery cat, he's called the hidden paw
For he's the master criminal who can defy the law
He's the bafflement of Scotland Yard, the Flying Squad's despair
For when they reach the scene of crime Macavity's not there !
Macavity, Macavity, there's no one like Macavity
He's broken every human law, he breaks the law of gravity

That sounded just like Prime Nutter Boris but perhaps Magpie Dick Turpin would be better singing that.

"I am a reformed character," Dick said. "I am a reformed character after Woodpile."

What was I going to sing ? Which cat could I be ?

"Albert you can be Mr Mistoffelees," Sammy suggested. "You'll be good at that."

You ought to ask Mr. Mistoffelees, the original Conjuring Cat
The greatest magicians have something to learn
From Mr. Mistoffelees' Conjuring Turn

It was great fun but Woodpile was fading into legend and I doubt half a million people would watch our version of the musical Cats. The Beatles suggested the apples could remain on the trees and not be turned into a DVD.

Wiggle's Summer School, will there be a Wiggle's Autumn School ? Wiggley's Winter School ? What classes will I take next time ?

RED KITE AIRWAYS:

B, B and C did not report on Wiggley's Summer School and ignored Cats. I've told you, have I not, that none of them can see anything beyond the end of their beaks. Uncharacteristically our Red Kites did not put it on Sky.

Red Kites, two of them good people but none of us really knew them all that well, what were their names ? Rupert and Murdoch perhaps ? That was a good guess, our Red Kites are Rupert Brandon and Richard Murdock. So we have a number of Richards here in Gardonia, Richard Robin the painter, Richard Turpin poacher turned gamekeeper. Richard This and Richard That, now we have Richard the Other.

It was on a rare occasion that Rupert and Richard landed on the ground instead of soaring high in the sky.

"We are starting something new," Rupert said.

"Something we know you will all want to use."

Use ? Use what ?

"We are launching an air passenger service, Red Kite Airways."

This was interesting, I turned up the volume on my snail ears.

"So I can learn to fly in the sky like you do ?"

"No, we will do the flying, you will simply ride on our backs on Red Kite Airways."

"You will not be flying to the european disunion," Boris said. His was more of an observation than a question.

"We are planning to fly out over the Atlantic Ocean ?"

The Atlantic Ocean, what is that ? Is it in Amazonia somewhere ?

"From Gardonia," Richard said, "you will be the first to fly the Atlantic, you will be Virgin Atlantics."

"I may give it a try," Boris said."

"I am not sure," Rupert cast doubt upon this particular passenger. "I am not sure we have a strong enough seat belt to hold your scamperings."

"I can sit still," I said. "I am known for it."

"I could sit still if I wanted to," Wiggley Woo added.

"Richard we have our first two passengers."

"Indeed we do Rupert."

I rode with Rupert, Wiggley rode on Flight R K001 with Richard.

"Gentlemen please ensure your seatbelts are securely fastened, your tables are safely stowed and seats in the upright position. Please observe the no smoking signs, smoking is not permitted until we have reached our cruising altitude."

I do not smoke and, neither as I am aware, does Wiggley Woo. I have never seen his twisting and turning to include a roll up.

When god made snails he forgot one thing, he should have given us wings. This was spectacular.

"We are the Red Kites," Rupert called back to me. "But we have cousins who call themselves Red Arrows. Hold on tight and allow me to show you how they fly."

Oh my goodness gracious me. We climbed up high then turned back towards the ground, twisting and turning. Climbing back up we suddenly turned upside down. It was exciting but for a snail it was scary. I wondered what Wiggley was making of it. I tried to look across to Richard but sweeping and soaring around in the sky it was not easy to see him.

Then as we slowed down I could see my friend, with neither of us having hands we waved to each other using our smiles. Red Kite Airways was going to be a success, that was certain. Rupert and Richard then effortlessly floated over fields and trees, over rivers and hills. All of this was Amazonia, what a big and far reaching place it was. I do not wear a watch although I can tell the time. Time ceased to exist onboard Red Kite Airways.

"Are you enjoying your flight ?" Rupert asked.

I was.

"Ladies and gentlemen we are about to commence our final approach, please return your seats to the upright position, close your tables and make sure your seat belt is tightly fastened. Oh, and one more thing; even if you do not smoke the no smoking sign is now turned on so please extinguish your cigarettes and do not light up again until you have passed through the arrivals hall."

Although they had previously been indifferent back on the ground B, B and C were clamouring for an interview. The queue of people wanting to book tickets with Red Kite Airways for flights was huge. Ladybirds and butterflies can themselves dance in the air but nothing like that Wiggley and I had just experienced.

Jake, Sir Jake The Dog, and Samuel had been watching. "Could we book tickets ?"

Rupert thought, Richard thought. Their conclusion was the same. "You would need to lose quite a few pounds in weight."

"But I am the catalog for Spike's Cave so it is my duty to sample everything before it is put on sale."

Where was Nutter Boris ? It would have been usual for him to have been scampering around after such an event.

"He has gone to visit his aunt," Jeremy Crowbinned. "I objected but he did not listen."

"Where does his aunt live ?"

"In Brazil where the nuts come from."

"Does Red Kite Airways fly there ?"

"We'll have to think about it," Richard said.

That was Richard Murdock, Richard The Robin was there with his paint and easel to record the event.

"Can we speak with you ?" B, B and C asked.

And so it was that B, B and C advertised Sky.

Jake did not manage to lose weight in order to fly with Red Kite Airways but Samuel managed it by a cat's whisker.

On his return Sammy said, "I am such a happy little cat, who needs a smart phone when you are happy."

Wiggley took me to one side. "I have something I want to say to you Albert," he said.

I wondered what he could possibly have to say. I was soon to find out.

"I am going to resign," Wiggley said. "When Boris returns I am going to tender my resignation ?"

"As Cabinet Secretary ?"

"Yes, I am going to become a writer, an author."

"What are you going to write ?"

"A novel, I am going to write a novel entitled The Flying Worm."

"But what about Cabinet Secretary ? Who will be the Cabinet Secretary ?"

"You are my friend. Albert The Snail and Cabinet Secretary."

L'ESCARGOT ALBERT ET L'ESCARGOT ALMA:
"I am not sure if I need to record this in a cabinet report," I said. "I am new to the job. The Prime Nutter will be back this afternoon, can you not wait until his return ?"

"We need to report it," B, B and C informed.

"We need to cancel our flights immediately," Rupert said.

"It's only for one day," Richard explained. "back to normal tomorrow."

"What is the emergency ?"

"It is not an emergency but due to Brexit all traffic is parked up on the M20, nothing can get through." Jake The Dog stepped into the conversation. "We have things ordered on Amazon which we need to collect."

"We'll need to cancel all flights today," Rupert said, "bring everything up from Kent, stop and then resume our schedule tomorrow,"

What should I write down. Why had I agreed to be Cabinet Secretary ?

Then everything started to happen.

Red Kite Airways landed, Sir Doggie Jake assisted by Samuel started to process the Amazon delivery.

"We have a passenger on board," Rupert advised. "She is going to need your help."

"Who and why is the help of the Cabinet Secretary needed ?"

"Not as Cabinet Secretary but as Albert The Snail. She is a refugee from the european disunion. She was about to be boiled in a french snail stew but managed to escape. She is Alma The Snail but only speaks french, she will need an interpreter, she will need an English teacher."

But I do not speak french, not any more. I only speak English.

I was contemplating this matter when His Royal Highness Prince Albert buzzed in. "My wife requests and requires you convene a special cabinet meeting at four o'clock this afternoon."

"But Prime Nutter Boris is away at the moment."

"He is returning, he is on his way right now."

"From Brazil ?"

"He has not been to Brazil, he has been to receive an award for Gardonia and will bring it to this afternoon's cabinet meeting."

"Yes, Your Royal Highness."

"Albert, Albert The Snail not you Your Royal Highness," Red Kite Richard said, "allow me to introduce you to Alma The Snail."

"Bonjour Alma, je suis Albert l'escargot." That took every bit of French language I had within my brain to say that.

B, B and C, I really did not need their beaks poking in at that time. Yes, they would need to report on the cabinet meeting but I knew nothing more than His Royal Highness had just said and was not going to speculate. Wiggley why did you resign ? Couldn't you be Cabinet Secretary and an Amazon novelist at the same time ?

"Merci Monsieur Albert. Je vous suis tres reconnaissant de votre gentilesse." Alma said.

What was that all about ?

"J'ai vraiment hate d'apprendre a parler agnlais."

Whatever Alma had just said I replied. "Oui – yes. Oui – yes." I had just taught our new resident her first word of English.

"Can you not give us an off the record comment ?" B as in B, B and C said.

"Non – No. Non – No." I had just taught Alma her second word of English.

Oh for goodness sake ! In all of this Nutter Boris returned from Brazil,   or   Timbuktu or Llanfairpwllgwyngyllgogerychwyrndrobwllllantysiliogogogoch or wherever he had been.

"Congratulations," Boris said. "I have been told of Wiggley's retirement and of your stepping in to the role. I look forward to working with you."

I am not sure that I looked forward to working with Boris. I introduced Alma to Boris.

"Je suis Neureux de vous reconterer. Je suis Boris. B-O-R-I-S, Boris." Boris taught Alma her third word of English.

Boris speaking french ! Was that politically correct for our Prime Nutter to be speaking a language from the european disunion ?

Her Majesty Queen Bee attended the cabinet meeting as Boris explained Gardonia and all of us who live here had won The Biodiversity Gold Medal. What an honour. Everyone spontaneously broke into singing our national anthem.

On the wings of a snow white dove
We bring you our peace and love
A sign from above
On the wings of a dove

When trouble surrounds us

When sadness comes
The body grows weak
The spirit grows numb
When these things beset us
Please do not forger
Our peace and our love
On the wings of a dove

On the wings of a snow white dove
We bring you our peace and love
A sign from above
On the wings of a dove

Gardonia where we all live had been awarded The Biodiversity Gold Medal.

"I thoroughly agree," Jeremy Crowbin said. "I thoroughly agree."

"As part of the award," Boris continued, "I have here a packet of sunflower seed which we will plant all around the realm. They will grow into a forest of happy smiling flowers."

"We are most certainly amused," Queen Bee Victoria said.

Life for this little snail was complicated, I was a busy little snail. Could I, should I, retire and become a writer ? What could I write to publish on Amazon ? An English french dictionary ? I don't think so. How about An Immigrant's Guide To Living In Our Garden, perhaps.

"I learned a new word today," Alma said. "Sammy taught me to say meow."

I smiled then said, "Let me teach you how to say smile."

It was time for me to expand Alma's vocabulary. "Would you allow me to change your name from Mademoiselle Alma to

Madam Albert ? Would you allow me to change my name from Monsieur Albert to Monsieur Alma ?"

"You mean from Miss Alma to Mrs Albert ? That would make me a very happy snail."

"Just one more word," this happy snail then said, "that word is kiss. Allow me to demonstrate its meaning.

Beppo here again:
As you probably guessed David aka Max wrote that story when Boris Johnson was Prime Minister, he later left 10 Downing Street to join the circus. I am not sure if he wanted to be a clown or an acrobat !

And all this Amazon stuff, it is Amazon that publishes my friend's writing. David, I mean Max, published that adventure on the first of January twenty, twenty-one. Not a single chocolate anywhere in sight.

And Beppo yet again:
Did you recognise some of our chocolate adventure characters appearing with Albert, minus their chocolates of course ? When you read David Max's next story see if they peep in again.

Amazon published my friend's story, the one following, on the twenty-third of February twenty, twenty-two.

Read on. (Well you wouldn't read *off* would you !) Off you go………..

THE ADVENTURES OF DOROTHY THE DUCK AND FRIENDS
By Max Robinson

AUTHOR'S NOTE:

This story is set in The National Trust's Stowe Gardens near Buckingham, England. At two hundred and fifty acres and the work of Lancelot Capability Brown Stowe it was once the home of The Duke of Buckingham.

Dorothy really does exist ! I'll not tell you where to find her, you can explore and seek her out yourself when you visit Stowe but trust me she is there !

Finally: This is not a book for children nor is this a book for grownups, this is a book for families. As you read through the different adventures please chat amongst yourselves and put your family into the story. Try to come up with adventures of your own where you can invite Dorothy to bring her friends and join in the fun.

Something more. As you read through the story you may find some little eccentricities you may not understand, odd words and phrases. For example why is Aaron's surname Lofting and why is Freddie a fox on the swim ? These are designed to send you off on tangent adventures as you try to fathom them out. Have fun and enjoy. Have fun and SMILE.

THE ROYAL VISIT:

"Thank you friends, thank you one and all." Bob said. "Thank you for coming together to remember and to honour my Uncle Robert."

"How long had he been Mayor of Stowe Park ?" Cyril asked.

"He took office the year before Queen Victoria and Prince Albert came to visit The Duke of Buckingham in 1845," Bob the Badger explained.

"Blimey !" Cyril the Cygnet exclaimed. "How many years ago is that ? I am not even one year out of the egg yet."

"One hundred and seventy-seven years," Hoot the Wise Owl did the adding up.

"It was a good innings for him then ," Simon the Squirrel said.

"He did not play cricket, he was a football man," Bob explained. "A Sheffield Wednesday supporter in actual fact. And if he hadn't forgotten to put his glasses on he would have seen the car coming and so would not have been run over."

"Was he wearing his hearing aid ? Didn't he hear it coming ? Had he forgotten that as well ?"

"No, he was wearing his hearing aid but it made no difference. The car was one of those new-fangled electric things so even Bertie the Bat would not have heard it speeding up Stowe Avenue."

"I can get my family to dig holes under the road meaning Stowe Avenue would break up and slow the cars down," Martin the Mole offered.

"And I'll get my family," Simon said, "to rip off the car windscreen wipers then you Freddie can report them to the police for being unroadworthy."

Freddie the Fox said he would take on the task.

"That Martin, that Simon, that Freddie will be for the new mayor to decide."

"But surely you will inherit you Uncle Robert's office Bob ?"

"Stowe has had a badger as its mayor for one hundred and seventy-seven years as Hoot explained, I think it is time for a change. A species other than a mammal if you all agree, feathers perhaps instead of fur ?"

"I sleep during the day," Hoot said, "I am a night owl so I do not think I would make a very good mayor."

"I was thinking of Dorothy," Bob said, "Mayor Dorothy the Duck."

Dorothy's bill blushed bright red.

"So Friends would you agree ?"

"Cyril the Cygnet, you are the youngest here, does Dorothy have your vote."

"She does."

"Hoot the Owl ?"

"I think it would be very wise for Dorothy to have my vote."

"Martin the Mole ?"

"If Dorothy becomes our mayor I will dig twice as many holes."

"And I'll rip off twice as many wipers," Simon the Squirrel said in support of a new lady mayor.

"Red the Kite ?"

"Ma'am I would be proud to serve under your aquatic wing."

"Freddie the Fox ?"

"I will continue as Stowe Park's chief of police if that is what Mayor Dorothy wishes."

"We have only one policeman, I mean police fox," Bob said, "which means Stowe Park's Chief of Police is actually a constable."

"Exactly," Freddie grinned, "Chief Constable."

"Finally, Bertie the Bat would you support Dorothy for mayor ?"

"Indeed I do."

"So it is unanimous then, Dorothy the Duck takes over from Badger Uncle Robert as Lady Mayor of Stowe Park."

"I think I need to go for a swim," Dorothy said.

Dorothy had her swim which began a celebration where all friends partied until the sun began to set, even Hoot kept his eyes open and danced about the trees. Finally, with the exception of Hoot and Bertie who would keep their night watch across the vast park everyone made their way to bed. Dorothy always slept on an island in the lake, Bob had his sett, Martin the Mole his hole, Freddy his den.

Everyone had their own special place of slumber, everyone would sleep deeply that night, everyone would dream and everyone would dream the same dream.

"I do not believe we are seeing what we are seeing," Prince Albert said. "That duck has just curtseyed to Your Majesty."

Standing on the path alongside the lake Dorothy had indeed politely made her anatidae bow to Great Britain's Queen Victoria and her consort Prince Albert of Saxe-Coburg and Gotha. Victoria returned the compliment, bending over to stroke Dorothy on top of her head.

"This parkland is a lovely place," Victoria said to Albert. "unlike the self-important residence of The Duke ! We live in Buckingham, Buckingham Palace and not some mere duke of an obscure county within One's realm !"

"We live in Buckingham Palace," Prince Albert corrected, "The Duke of Buckingham lives in Stowe House."

"We are not amused !" Queen Victoria scoffed.

"Well I am amused," Albert smiled, "I am amused by this lovely duck."

Dorothy was joined by Simon the Squirrel who amidst his scampering tried to raise his right squirrel-paw as a salute the royal couple. Her Majesty was amused.

"You have met our Mayor Dorothy," Simon said.

"You can speak !" Prince Albert was astonished.

"Of course I can, I am a squirrel."

"And I am a fox," Freddie joined the group. "I am in charge of security here in our park so I will be looking after you during your stay."

"We are having a bit of a get together in Squirrel Wood," Simon said. "Would our royal quests like to come along ?"

Before either could answer Mayor Dorothy spoke. "Squirrel Wood ! That's a long way to walk."

"You have wings," Simon countered, "fly !"

"You can ride on my back Freddie offered."

Walking, Flying or riding on Freddie's back Dorothy did not particularly fancy a trip all the way to Squirrel Wood and so decided to wake up from her dream. The others followed their mayor's lead and so bade farewell to Stowe Park's royal visitors.

THE WAR OF THE WORMS:
"How can a duck be a vegetarian." Freddie's words were rhetorical, a statement rather than a question.

"Well I don't eat worms !" Dorothy replied confirming her dietary status. "When I dip my head below the water it is to eat weed and not wriggling worms."

"You should try them," Freddie continued. "Worms on toast with a side-serving of pineapple."

"From where pray am I supposed to get a pineapple ? I've not seen any growing in Stowe Park."

"Nick it from the Duke's kitchen, he's got more than he can eat and now Queen Victoria has left early there's bound to be some left over."

"Chief Constable Freddie the Fox you are supposed to be in charge of security, not breaking and entering !"

"I found one while digging a hole," Martin said. "It didn't taste very nice, a bit like garlic. A worm that is not a pineapple."

"A French worm !"

It was not a French invertebrate that came to join the conversation. "My name is Wiggley, Wiggley Woo, I thought I should come along. I am worried about the invasion of alien worms."

"The garlic worms ?" Martin asked.

"I've never eaten garlic," Wiggley Woo wriggled, "they tell me it is not very nice and these garlic worms are not very nice either."

"Tell us more," Dorothy said.

"My fellow worms and I wriggle our way through the soil making it a better place for things to grow but these alien worms pollute the soil which makes it hard for anything to grow. Eventually even the trees will die."

"Some of these trees are hundreds of years old," Simon was concerned. "I know, I scamper through them every day."

"And my family makes nests in them," Red the Kite said. "What will we do without Stowe Park's trees ?"

"We need to undertake an investigation," Freddie explained. "We need to find out who these worms are and where they come from. I'll be in charge."

"I am not sure it will help your investigation," Hoot began, "I am not sure your investigation will be any help anyway but at night I have seen some strange lights coming from the sky and landing here in the park"

"I cannot see," Bertie said, "but I have sensed those lights, they come down with a silent supersonic flash."

"Are you saying the lights have something to do with alien worms ?" Wiggley asked.

Hoot did not directly answer the question but in posing question for Wiggley Woo gave indication of his thinking. "Are you and the Woo Family within Stowe Park able to communicate with the alien worm invaders ? Can you speak to them directly or do you need a phone to call their home ?"

Wiggley Woo did not know what a phone was.

Dorothy put on her mayoral thinking cap. "Perhaps we should go and take a nap, rest then tonight we can all stay awake to keep watch for the lights."

"Good idea, let's all put on our night caps."

"If we spot where one lands and if we find worms there we can then decide our next step."

"Or next wiggle," Woo said, "not a step but a wiggle."

And so it was that night with Bertie the Bat and Hoot the Owl flying in the night sky all other friends, under the direction of

Freddie the Fox, not that anyone took much notice of him, patrolled the park looking for landing areas.

The lights were coming from a hole in space, what science fiction writers may call a worm hole and an astrophysicist refer to as an event horizon. Each flash was made by one alien worm, what the team began to name an Earth Terrorist. Within micro seconds of landing the aliens, ET, were underground contaminating the soil.

"We'll never catch them," Martin the Mole said.

"And if we did catch them what would we do with them ?" Wiggley Woo asked

"Toast ? Pineapple ?" Was Freddie the Fox's thought, a thought which everyone dismissed with Dorothy's earlier words.

"I am a vegetarian duck," Dorothy reminded everyone. "What we have got to do is to find a way not to kill these Earth Terrorists but to induce them to return to where they came from."

"ET go home !" Everyone said in unison.

"While I was up in the night sky," Bertie said, "my senses told me there is a major storm on the horizon."

High winds are common at Stowe Park, usually Bertie did not comment but hung tightly upside down in a tree until things were calmer.

"This is going to be a big one so everyone be careful. Simon no scampering about the trees and those of you with wings keep them folded."

"I will be underground," Martin said. "Avoiding ET of course but safe underground."

"I'll keep you company," Wiggley Woo offered.

"And I'll be in my set under the tree," Bob added. "That tree has stood for five hundred years so no huff and puff of wind will blow my house down."

But a puff, even without a huff, of wind did blow Bob the Badger's house down.

Wednesday 18th February 1520 Queen Elizabeth was on the throne of England. She ordered that land owners up and down the realm were to plant oak trees which in future years could be cut down to make ships in order to conquer new lands, to repel enemies and keep England safe from invasion. Bob's Oak was one of those trees which somehow Queen Elizabeth and the navy overlooked.

Bob's Oak did not manage to repel the invasion of ET. The alien worms had damaged the soil so rendering this ancient tree unstable in the ground. As the storm hit Queen Elizabeth royal proclamation was torn apart.

"Where am I to live now ?" Bob said. "I have lived there since I was a baby boar. I am now homeless !"

"We are all your friends," Dorothy said. "You will never be homeless while we are here."

"I will scamper around every single tree here in Stowe Park, every one of the twenty-six thousand, four hundred and thirty-two until I find the finest home in the land for you," Simon promised.

"And I will check underground to make certain the roots of all twenty-six thousand, four hundred and thirty-two are secure," Martin the Mole assured his friend.

"Twenty-six thousand, four hundred and thirty-one," Dorothy corrected, "now that Bob's Oak has fallen."

"And I will wiggle my way around every tree undertaking a worm survey," Wiggley offered. "ET be ready for me to count you."

There were no worms for Wiggley to count. ET appeared to have gone home.

"Perhaps the wind blew the aliens away, hopefully back through their worm holes."

"I have found the perfect home for you," Simon the Squirrel smiled. "Wiggley and Martin have checked it out so you can move in as soon as you like. It is a beech tree, a copper beech tree. Bob's Copper Beech Tree."

"If it is a copper beech then it naturally comes with my protection as Stowe Park's number one copper !" Freddie assured.

"Even so," Red said, "My family and I will make our nest in its branches to keep an eye on you."

So had the alien worms really gone ? Had ET truly gone home ? Had they been swept back up into space by the storm ? The friends agreed they needed to ensure no repeat invasion ever took place. But how could that be achieved ?

"Blocking, sealing the wormholes is what we must to. That has to be accomplished but surely it is a task even our very own Bertie the Bat, Bertie would find hard to undertake."

"I will do it Bertie assured, even Hell itself will not stop me."

"Hell ? Bertie the Bat Outa Hell."

"More Bertie the Bat Into Hell."

"What do we seal it with, the wormhole ? Concrete ?"

"That would be far too heavy for me to carry," Bertie explained. "I am only a little bat after all."

"And we need something the alien worms would want to eat so not move out to build a second entry point," Wiggley explained.

"But what happens when they have eaten the plug ? What happens then ?"

"I will have to go back and refill it, I guess this going to have to become a regular bat-mission."

Chief Constable Freddie was listening carefully, he would not be flying to the edge of space himself but technically he was in charge. "So what can our resident bat outa hell take with him to plug the wormhole ? Some meat perhaps ? I know a meatloaf ?"

"As I have explained," Mayor Dorothy said, "I am a vegetarian duck so I could not give that idea my support."

"What about a nut roast ?" Simon the Squirrel suggested. "I could most certainly collect all the nuts needed for that. A nutloaf, would that work Billy the Bat Outa, I mean Into, Hell ?"

THE STOWE PARK OLYMPICS:

"Sometimes," *Mr* Dorothy the Duck said, "I feel the way Prince Albert and The Duke of Edinburgh must have felt. Serving my wife's office always one paddle behind her but I have an idea I hope you will all like."

"And what Sir is that idea ?" Martin the Mole asked.

"Please do not call me Sir, I am an ordinary duck just like you."

"But I am a mole, I am not a duck. I am a mole and I live in a hole."

"Indeed." Mr Dorothy Duck blushed as he moved on to explain his idea. "Cyril the Cygnet you are the youngest member of the Stowe Park Family so I want you to help me with my idea."

"Me ? But I am just an ugly duckling."

"You are not a ducking but a cygnet and ugly you are not, very soon you will be the most handsome living thing in all of the park ?"

"Just what is it you are going on about my Dear Husband ?" Dorothy asked. "What is your idea ?"

"We are going to stage The Stowe Olympic Games."

"Sounds a good idea but what kind of games are you talking about and what is an Olympic ?"

"I swim and so does my wife your Mayor."

"We paddle Dear and we can also waddle on the ground."

"Indeed. How do the rest of you move about Stowe Park ?"

"I wriggle," Woo said.

"I'm a miner, I dig holes," Martin said, "But I've never found any gold nor even so much as a lump of coal for that matter."

"That's because we are not in California and this is not 1849. Neither is Margaret Thatcher Prime Minister nor Arthur Scargill the leader of NUM."

What was Mr Duck talking about ?

"I fly," Red explain.

"And I scamper," Simon said.

"Me ? I run," Freddie said, "I am a fox on the run."

"I guess I badger," Bob said, "if there is such a thing as badgering."

"And I'm as blind as a bat," Bertie said, "so I radar."

"Wiggling, swimming, paddling, walking, burrowing, flying, running, badgering or radaring I want each and every person to pick an alternative way to move then spend a week practicing before meeting here where we will all race each other."

"So if a fox learns to swim is that olympicing ? Fox on the swim and not fox on the run, I see."

"If I shut my eyes as I leap from one tree to another would that be batting rather than scampering. That would be a bat outa hell !"

"Leave hell outa this, that was in a different adventure."

Wiggley Woo had been thinking. "I don't have any legs," he said, "so wouldn't it be better to have Stowe Paralympics ?"

"I have a list of events which Cyril will assist me by writing them on leaves which he will post on Bob's Tree then you can all sign up for everything that takes your fancy."

Simon, Martin, Bob, Freddie and Wiggley Woo put their names down for the Lake Freestyle Swim. Hoot was appointed Official Starter and Swim Judge. Cyril would be the official time keeper.

"Take your marks – get set - HOOT !"

Flying above the lake Red the Kite gave the spectators a running commentary.

"And Simon's dive into the water gives him an initial lead but the scamper stroke is perhaps not proving quite as effective as we had all expected. Now Freddie after a Sweet dive is definitely overtaking Simon and must be the favourite, Freddie the Fox on the swim. But wait, coming up on the outside not wiggling but with a powerful woo glide here comes Wiggley. This is going to be a close race."

Indeed it was. Standing on the podium Simon the Squirrel took Bronze with Wiggley Woo is second place. Trying to find a neck about which to hang the Stowe Olympics Lake Freestyle Swim Dorothy awarded him the Silver medal. On top of the podium, waving to all was Sweet Freddie the Fox, the fox on the swim.

So what came next ? The three legged race. However, only Cyril the Cygnet signed up to race. As Mayor Dorothy was not herself participating it meant Cyril had nobody to tie a leg to.

"I'll put two of my legs in my pocket," Mole offered, "then tie one of the free legs to Cyril."

And so it was. As the only participants at the end of their one hundred yard stumble Cyril the Cygnet and Martin the Mole won all three medals; Bronze, Silver and Gold !

In deference to Dorothy the egg and spoon race became the nut and spoon race. Then the runcible spoon race.

"And Martin the Mole is in the lead," Red began his commentary. "But wait, here comes Simon the Squirrel, no wait he is running backwards. It's over this way you nutter ! Racing to the finish line it is our very own Bertie the Bat."

Just three events in the first ever Stowe Park Olympics. With Bertie winning gold in the blindfold runcible nut and spoon race, Freddie coming in silver there was no bronze award. It took more than an hour to locate Simon running backwards.

Accepting defeat Simon announced. "I think we should have one more event, *Simon Says. Clap your hands in the air, do it double time, slow it down like before.*"

"I think we should leave that until the snowdrops bloom," Mr Dorothy the Stowe Olympic Organiser replied. "We'll save that for the Winter Olympics."

LITTLE BOY LOST:
"This is an emergency, a red emergency," Freddie the Fox said to Simon the Squirrel. "I need you to scamper round the park and tell everyone to meet at Bob's Tree."

"What's happened ? What's the emergency ?"

"There's a little boy who is lost in the park, Bob the Badger is looking after him, we need to find his parents. The little boy is lost."

"I'll scamper," Simon said.

Simon's scamper was a super-scamper as he brought everyone to join Bob and the lost little boy.

"I am Dorothy," Dorothy said. "What is your name my little friend ?"

"I am Aaron," he replied. "Autistic Aaron."

"Autistic, that's an unusual name," Freddie said.

Hoot hooted telling Freddie to be quiet. If a fox did not know what autistic meant a wise owl did.

"We are your friends Aaron," Dorothy said. "How old are you ?"

"Seven," Aaron replied. "Seven years and twenty-six days, two and a half hours."

"Aaron has lost his Mum and Dad," Bob told the assembled friends. "They were walking round the lake but when they took the path up the hill to the trees Aaron ran on ahead and became separated from his parents."

"They must be worried," Red said. "I'll take to the sky and fly round looking for them."

"Don't worry," Cyril the Cygnet said putting a wing around Aaron's shoulder Red will find your Mum and Dad."

"I didn't know that animals could speak," Aaron said.

"All animals speak," Dorothy replied. "Or perhaps when it comes to ducks you could say we quack."

"I speak but I also wiggle," said Woo."

"All animals speak," Hoot spoke wisely, "but not all human people listen so do not hear what we are saying."

"I am listening," Arron assured. "When I speak people do not usually listen to me so most of the time I do not bother to speak."

"That sounds wise to me," Hoot said.

He did not share his wisdom but Hoot wondered how they would tell Aaron's Mum and Dad they had found their lost son if they did not listen to anything spoken to them.

"Don't worry," Cyril said, "we are all your friends and I promise you we will find your Mum and Dad. "When you are with them again perhaps you may like to sit on my back and I'll take you for a ride on our lake."

"I'd like that," Aaron smiled. It was unusual for him to smile but he found he liked it and would now be doing it more often.

"What is that bird doing ?" Mrs Lofting said. "It keeps swooping down."

"It's as if it wants us to follow it, "Mr Lofting, Aaron's father said. "Am I being silly or is it trying to get us to follow it ? Do you think it knows where Aaron is ?"

"Aaron, Aaron darling," Mrs Lofting shouted, "where are you ? Mummy and Daddy are looking for you."

Red landed on the ground right in front of them, hoped for a few yards before flying back up into the air.

"Aaron darling where are you ?"

"Over there, look there's a fox."

"He's got a squirrel sitting on his back."

"And there's a worm on top of the squirrel's head."

Freddie, Simon and Wiggley joined Red in trying to show Mr and Mrs Lofting the way to their son.

"Hugh I really think we should follow them all."

"Aaron where are you ?"

"He is not going to answer you," Hugh said. "Our son is autistic."

"I'm over here," Aaron called back excitedly. "Where have you been ?"

"We've been looking for you. What have you been doing ?"

"I've been talking with my friends."

"Friends ? What friends ?"

"Hugh he is talking, our son is talking. Listen."

Mr Lofting was listening but was finding it hard to believe his ears.

"Of course I am talking, I've been talking with my friends I told you." Aaron smiled.

"What friends ?"

Dorothy stepped forward. "Mr and Mrs Lofting, your son Aaron has been talking to the animals. Please allow me to introduce you to us all."

"What ?"

"Listen to her Mum."

"I am Dorothy and I am a duck, this is my husband Mr Duck. Cyril the Cygnet is the one with his wing about your son. Red the Kite found you then asked Freddie the Fox, Simon the Squirrel and Wiggley the Worm to help him bring you here. This is Bob the Badger, it is home we are here gathered outside. In Bob's Tree above your head is Hoot the Owl and poking his nose up out of the ground is Martin the Mole."

"You can speak ?"

"All animals can speak Mr Lofting, it just requires humans to listen to them."

"Mr and Mrs Lofting, my name is Cyril I just want to say that your little boy is amazing, Amazing Aaron. I would like to take him for a ride on my back, a ride on the lake if you will let me."

"I am dreaming."

"No you are not Mum, can I go for a ride on the lake with Cyril please ?"

"Let him."

"We planned a special day out" Hugh Lofting said as he waved to his son on the lake. "It has been a long drive from where we live in Wiltshire, Puddleby-on-the-Marsh all the way to this park."

"Has it been a special day ?"

"You could say that. Do you think that Cyril is strong enough to give me a lake ride as well."

"I'm not sure about that, perhaps you should come back when he is a fully grown swan."

"You can ride on my back and we can have a wiggle together if you like," Woo said.

DOROTHY'S DIAMOND:
"You've found my ring !"

Martin the Mole had indeed found a ring while burrowing through the ground at Stowe Park but who was this person, this strange looking person and what was he doing at Stowe ? Why was he saying it was his ring ? Probably a good idea to ask him.

"Who are you ?"

"I am Brown, Lancelot Brown and I am the head gardener here on the estate."

Mole's mind filled with questions, in which order should he ask them ?

"I have lived here all my life since I was a mini-mole and I've never seen you before."

"I though the word for an infant mole was a pup rather than mini. Such an expression sounds a bit Issigonis to me."

What was this man talking about ? Better move on to the next question but whoever Lancelot Brown was he had not responded to Mole saying he had never seen him before. That actually was not a question so perhaps Martin needed to rearticulate it. But he didn't.

"Lancelot ? Wasn't he something to do with a lake and King Arthur ? I found your ring by our lake."

"I am not Sir Lancelot from Arthurian Legend but Lancelot Brown and my monarch is King George. I was head gardener at Stowe and you appear to have found my ring."

"Yes, I found it over there by the lake ! So it is the ring of the lake."

"What's happening here ?" Chief Constable Freddie arrived. "Who is this and what is that thing on his head ?"

Lancelot Brown raised a hand which he placed on top of his head. "I am Lancelot Capability Brown and this is my dress wig. I am the architect of Stowe Park, I was its chief gardener."

"I am Chief Constable Freddie the Fox and I am in charge of security here at Stowe."

"Actually he is the only constable," Mole said. "You said you were a gardener, now you say you were an architect. Before I give you back your ring I will need a better explanation that that. And what that word you used earlier, issigonis ?"

"He designed the Eifel Tower," Freddie said. "Issigonis did."

No he didn't. Who were these crazy animals ? All Lancelot Brown wanted was to have back his long lost ring. Something was needed in the situation enabling Lancelot Sensibility Brown to have the diamond ring back on his finger.

When Hoot had understood and assessed the situation he apologised to the park's visitor then sent Freddie to gather all friends and bring them to meet Mr Brown.

"He will be as quick as he can," Hoot apologised but we may need to be patient. "Bertie will be asleep so he'll have to be woken up and Wiggley isn't the fastest runner in the park."

"Perhaps Simon can give him a ride on his back," Martin suggested.

"I am Dorothy, Dorothy the Duck and Mayor of Stowe Park, I understand that Martin the Mole has found a ring you lost here a few years ago."

"Two hundred and eighty-one years ago to be precise Madam Mayor. It was a gold ring Your Duckship with a small diamond."

"Is that the ring you found Martin ?"

"Yes Your Quackship."

"Then please return it to its rightful owner."

Martin did as he was told. Lancelot Brown took the wig from his head and scratched his mind as he studied his long lost possession. He then wiped a tear from his eye. He used a handkerchief, not his wig.

"Thank you."

"We could think that you are a visitor to our home here in Stowe Park," Dorothy continued, "but it is we who are the visitors. This is your park, you created its beauty and we just live here. I would like to know and I am sure my friends would like to know, how you created such a beautiful place. Would you kindly tell us your story ?"

"Of course I will, I would be proud to tell you all. You are special people, very special people."

Wiping a second tear from his eye, this time using the toupee, then putting the wig onto the floor he sat down to begin. The gold which had been buried for so many years until Martin found it still shone and the diamond excitedly sparkled.

"I was born in August 1716 and fell in love with nature when I was but a small child. My father was a land agent in Northumberland and so I guess I was born to be a gardener. I joined Lord Cobham's gardening team here at Stowe in 1741 and later became head gardener. It was then I planned the landscape you all live in. Obviously I did not do everything myself, I drew up the plan and had a small army of gardeners helping me. Simon the trees you scamper through today I planted as tiny little saplings. As I did so I tried to imagine who would make their nests in the branches and who would make their homes digging under the roots. Mayor Dorothy the lake on which you paddle was once just a small stream but by changing the level of the ground your home was created, yours and of course Cyril's home."

"Thank you," Dorothy said.

"It was Lord Cobham, later to be The Duke of Buckingham, who paid for everything and as such I was working for him but it was for future generations of foxes, badgers, owls, bats, birds, moles and squirrels I was truly working."

"And worms," Wiggley Woo said. "Don't forget the worms."

"Of course. Without worms caring for the ground nothing would have grown."

When he had finished speaking everyone spontaneously applauded.

"So Madam Dorothy you are the Mayor of Stowe Park ?"

"Indeed."

"When I planned and developed this land for his Lordship never in my wildest dream could I have ever imagined such lovely people as you would make it your home."

Simon wanted to say they were animals not people in the humanoid sense but Hoot silently told him to keep his scampering mouth closed.

"You are our mayor but you do not wear a chain of office."

Dorothy shook her duck head.

Lancelot sensibility took the watch from his waistcoat pocket but it was not to look at the time. He disconnected it from its gold chain. With the watch back in its pocket he took the ring from his little finger, the sun caught the diamond sending a sparkle high above the trees. He then threaded the ring onto the watch chain before placing it around Mayor Dorothy's neck.

"You now have a chain of office."

"Thank you Mr Brown."

"Call me Lancelot, Lancelot of the Lake. As you wear it I will take pride in all that Stowe has and is every day achieving."

RIDERE AD MUNDUM:
"You are the oldest and the wisest member of our family," Cyril the Cygnet said.

"Wisdom is a compliment but I am not sure that old age is such," Hoot replied. Owls don't smile but deep inside he was doing just that. SMILING.

"I want to share an idea I have with you. You being the oldest and wisest member of our family and me being they youngest and most naive."

"I am not sure that naivety is a character trait I would associate with you young Cyril. So what is your idea ?"

"Now that Mayor Dorothy has a chain of office I have been thinking we perhaps need a family name. I am Cyril the Cygnet, you are Hoot the Owl. Then there is Bob the Badger, Simon the Squirrel, Red the Kite, Wiggley Woo the Worm, Freddie the Fox and Martin the Mole. Could we all perhaps have a family name, the same family name for us all ?"

Hoot liked what the family's most junior member was thinking. "Have you an idea for what that name could be ?"

"We all live in Stowe Park."

"Indeed we do."

"So first of all I thought of Parker but then I thought of a double name."

"A double name ?"

"Stoic-Parker."

"What does the word stoic mean young Cyril and where did you find it ?"

"I just made it up, it doesn't have a meaning."

"Oh yes it does fledgling Cyril, stoic means strong and sturdy, it means patient and tolerant, it means enduring. I think it would make a perfect family name. Cyril Stoic-Parker, Hoot Stoic-Parker, Simon Stoic-Parker, Freddie Stoic-Parker, Martin Stoic-Parker. I am not sure how easily Wiggley Woo Stoic-Parker rolls off the tongue, it's a bit of a double barrelled double barrel name but still we could get used to it and at our head is Mayor Dorothy Stoic-Parker."

"You like my idea Hoot ?"

"I don't like your idea Cyril, I LOVE it ! It makes me SMILE."

"Thank you."

"But first we have to share it with everyone and have Mayor Dorothy seek universal agreement. I will ask Simon Stoic-Parker soon to be to scamper round and gather everyone together."

No sooner said than done but Simon, would-be Simon Stoic-Parker, also assembled Lancelot Sensibility Brown, Sir Lancelot of Stoic Park Lake. Queen Victoria and Prince Albert happened to be passing again. Even the young Aaron Lofting joined the gathering. The Duke of Buckingham, however, did not attend, he was too busy guarding his kitchen. The man from Del Monte he say Freddie leave my pineapples alone.

Cyril was nervous when it came to explaining his renaming family members but with Hoot's support when Dorothy put it to the vote the motion was carried unanimously.

Her Majesty spoke. "It is but a trifle, a pineapple trifle perhaps, that the Duke was unable to join us and I have to say we are thoroughly amused. Cyril Stoic-Parker you know that the emblem for Buckingham is a swan."

Chief Constable Freddie Stoic-Parker thought it was an Agadoo Tree but he did not interrupt his Queen who even if she claimed to be amused would not be when he spoke.

"You are soon to become a swan Cyril. All swans glide across their water under my personal protection, the protection of the monarch. In a time yet to come my great-great-great-grandson will take on this responsibility. When he does you will become his lieutenant here in Stowe Park but right now you are my own special representative. Bow your head Cyril Stowe-Parker."

The young cygnet did as his monarch ordered.

"Arise your head Sir Cyril Stoic-Parker."

What !

"Yes," Her Majesty Queen Victoria confirmed, "the emblem of Buckingham is a swan. Sir Cyril I here charge you with the task of designing a coat of arms and maxim for the Stoic-Parker Family."

What !

"What is a maxim ?" Cyril asked when the royal party had left.

"It's a double helping of pineapple trifle," Aaron smiled. It was that smile which gave Cyril his idea.

"Billy Wobblestick did not write his plays in Latin," Hoot smiled.

"Who's Billy Wobblestick ?"

"William Shakespeare, he did not put Latin into the mouth of Romeo Montague even if he was living in Verona."

"Where is Verona and who is Romeo Montague ?"

"Never mind all that, Latin is a dead language. The Stoic-Parker family does not speak with words from a dead language. Just for your information if you did want our family motto to be written in Latin it would be Ridere Ad Mundum but it sounds much better when spoken as Smile At The World."

"It would sound even better," Cyril smiled, "if it was spoken Smile At The World And The World Will Smile Back At You."

Beppo here:
I like that: *The World Will Smile Back At You*. That's what we clowns do, we try to make people smile. I think that the word SMILE should be written in block capital letters. Did Dorothy and her friends make you SMILE, they did for me.

Beppo again:
BEPPO THE CLOWN A story for children written for grownups to read…

That's how my friend David began writing about our adventures. David is a prolific writer but Enid Blyton he is not, nor is he Roald Dhal. He would love to write stories for children but that's just not his way. Yes, many of his stories are for children but they are for grownups to read. That is how it is over the next twenty-four thousand, five hundred and fifty-words. To quote David: *This is a story about a child's life viewed from an adult's point of view.*

David wrote this story in 1985. Read and let it make you SMILE.

THE WILD ADVENTURES OF DI CENTRAL EATING

There are ten adventures, plural, but we begin with an adventure, single. This and the other nine are most certainly wild.

The Wild Adventure Of Di Central Eating
Di's First Fish
Platinum Plated Pitchforks
Pathfinders In Space
Rock And Roll Superstar
Nipper
Football Hooligan
The Great Trolley Race
And Then We Were Three
The Gypsy's Curse

Off you go then David Mr Max tell us just how wild Di's adventures are. **Beppo…**

THE WILD ADVENTURE OF DI CENTRAL EATING:

Let me begin by quite clearly explaining that my family is not Welsh.

My mother always claimed that our ancestors originated in France and fled to England at the time of the revolution. That may or may not be true, I don't know, to be honest I have my doubts. But of one thing I am certain and that is not a single drop of Celtic, Welsh blood flows in our veins. Not that I would have any objection to being of that nationality, no none at all, for they are a proud race and their soft, lilting tongue is a joy to listen to. But, sadly the Albons never have been and never will be Welsh so there's an end to it.

Then why is my brother called Di ?

I was just two years old when Brother David came along. Two years old, toddling and full of infant chatter, mispronounced words in a language all of my very own, well I guess I understood what I was on about at least. But my mother could not and try as she did she never managed to teach me to say *David*. In the end she gave up and settled for Di. Even today, within the close circle of our family, Brother David is still known as Di.

But what of Central Eating ?

Now, of course, you all know what central heating is don't you ? Lots of radiators all fed from one boiler keeping the entire house warm. Well something like that anyway. When I was a kid only the very rich had central eating and we weren't even ordinary rich. Every morning, before he went out to work, my father had to light the downstairs coal fire. He would scrunch up the previous day's newspaper, pile a wigwam of kindling wood about it then encircle the construction with lumps of coal. A match gave the initial light which Dad would fan and coax into a roaring blaze. Not that it worked perfectly every time, aborted attempts were common and were followed by the entire process being repeated: the newspapers, the kindling wood and the carefully selected coals. Those fires kept our lounge lovely and warm, with a back boiler heating the kitchen but the rest of the house was as cold as the grave. Di and I used to have competitions to see who could chip the biggest slithers of ice off the bedroom windows where the condensation froze overnight. That was central heating, or the lack of it, but Di was Central Eating.

The thing was when Di was about six years old his baby teeth started to fall out. Most children lose their baby, or milk, teeth as a gradual process over a number of years but Di lost four bottom teeth and three upper teeth in the space of a few months. All he had left at the front of his mouth was one stubborn peg that refused to budge. Poor old Di found it quite a handicap trying to eat. Munching at the side of his mouth proved impossible so all he could do was to trap whatever it was with this single, central tooth against his bottom gum. Hence Central Eating. I do not know where this name originated but until well after his mouth filled again with adult teeth David Albon was known to all as Di Central Eating.

Di and I used to attend Banners Gate County Primary School which took all children in the neighbourhood from the age of five years until they left at eleven. Those up to the age of eight were in the infant department while the older ones belonged to the juniors. the infants had their classrooms on the left hand side of the school and the juniors on the right, that was if you stood with your back to the headmistresses office and faced the hall. If you turned round then the infants were on the right and the juniors on the left. I expect you understand. In the middle were all the important parts of the school like the headmistresses room, the secretary's office, the hall, the dining room and, of course, the dreaded school kitchen.

Goodness how I hated school dinners and Di found eating anything near impossible. Thank the Lord we only had to stay one day a week. Like most mums in those days, our mum did not go out to work and was always at home to cook a midday meal for us. But Thursdays were different. Thursday was Young Wives Club at the local church and Mum, being on the committee, had to get things ready for the afternoon meeting with no time to make us lunch.

School dinners weren't exactly bad, they were diabolical consisting of the most fiendish menus. Tapioca pudding, boiled cabbage, swedes, cheese pie and toad in the hole with real live toads ! Of course the cooks were not working at all to prepare meals for the children, nobody thought that, but really for the local pig farmer.

You see after we had eaten our fill, which usually wasn't very much, all the scraps had to be tipped into the pig bin. This was a large metal dustbin, well more than one dustbin on most days, sometimes three on a bad day. At the of the meal these were wheeled outside to await the pig-man. He came, I think, every other day to take away all the full bins and leave empty ones for the next two days. I expect he had contracts with all the schools and that his pigs grew very fat on it all. Funny to think that when we eat bacon and egg we are really eating recycled cabbage and tapioca pudding. Makes you want to become Jewish doesn't it.

It was on the day the pig-man came that it happened, it must also have been a Thursday for I remember Di and I were to stop for school dinners. I had just passed into the junior department moving to the right, or was it the left, hand side of the school while Brother Di stayed in the infants on the other side. The juniors and infants had different morning and afternoon playtimes but during the lunch hour had to share the same playground. We older juniors would then try to take no notice of the infants, being careful to keep away from them. It simply was not done to be seen playing with babies now that we were eight years old.

The pig-man always came during the junior playtime, some of us on that day stood and watched as he drove his small pick-up truck across the playground ton the back door of the kitchen and the waiting pig bins. First of all he went and checked how many full bins there were. This he did by picking each bin up in turn and judge-weighing the contents. That day all six bins were full, a bumper collection. Very quickly the new clean bins were off-loaded and the full ones humped on to the back of the pick-up truck. Then he was off and we returned to our games.

A sharp blast of the teacher's whistle spelt the end of playtime and we lined up waiting to return to our classrooms. But something was up. Miss Evans, the headmistress, was at the front talking to the teacher on duty. Someone was in for it ! Mis Evans had the habit of talking to teachers while in the presence of children by placing a hand in front of her face and talking out the corner of her mouth. It made it quite impossible for us to hear what she was saying. But it was certain that at least one of us was in big trouble and every child present searched their memories for anything bad they had done over the last few weeks. What terrible discovery had Miss Evans made ?

"Richard Albon would you come with me please."

I looked round in panic. Richard Albon, that was me. Had she said my name or had I heard wrong ? What had I done ? Nothing, no nothing, she hadn't called my name at all. But she had. Miss G M Evans, Headmistress and demi-god of Banners Gate County Primary School was soon marching through the lines of children to collect me. My heart thumped and my legs turned to jelly. I would soon be dead, but what had I done ?

I had never before been inside Miss Evans office. Within an instant I took in every fine detail of the room. In fear I guess I was searching for where she kept her cane. As Miss Evans closed the door behind us I noticed Mrs Lewis was in the room sitting in the corner. Why on earth was she there ? She was Di's teacher. I was soon to find out.

"Have you seen David ?" She asked shakily.

"We walked to school together this morning," I explained. Perhaps it was Di who was in trouble and not me after all. I wondered what he had done and how, as his big brother, I could try to protect him.

"Have you seen him at all since then Richard ?" Miss Evans asked slowly, seating herself behind the big desk that dominated the room.

"No Miss Evans. What's he done ?"

"He's gone missing," Mrs Lewis blurted out. Miss E vans turned and scowled at her. It was evident the interruption was not appreciated.

"You didn't see him while you were out at playtime ?"

"No Miss Evans, he's still in the infants and I'm in the juniors now."

"I know that Richard but when Mrs Lewis took her class back after the infant playtime David wasn't with the other children."

"Perhaps he went to the toilet," I ventured.

"We've searched the toilets and now I've got prefects checking every classroom."

"His friends said he was playing hide and seek," Mrs Lewis spoke again, "and no one could find out where he was hiding."

"Thank you Mrs Lewis," Miss Evans scowled again. "I'll handle this. Do you think he may have gone home Richard ?"

"No, today's Thursday."

"Thursday ?"

"We stay to school dinners on a Thursday."

"But would that stop him from running off home ?"

I thought that school dinners gave the perfect excuse for anyone to run off anywhere but explained that Di could not possibly have gone home because he knew our mother would not be in."

"I think I'll ask the secretary to telephone home just in case," Miss Evans lifted the telephone receiver, placed a hand in front of her face and talked out the corner of her mouth. It must have been a permanent mannerism of hers for I could see no harm in my hearing her ask the school secretary to ring my Mum.

As soon as she had finished speaking there came a knock at the door. It was the prefects reporting back the results of their search. They had failed to locate Di. The secretary then came in to explain there had been no reply on our home telephone.

"Do you know where your mother will be ?"

I explained all about the young wives club, the committee and Mum having to be there early to get things ready.

Miss Evans paused sensing something terrible must have happened. She stood up, pacing her hand upon the desk, fingers spread and leaned upon them. "I want one more thorough search of the school and then I'm calling the police."

Of course, the search no matter how thorough did not find Di.

The police, sniffing a murder, or at the very least a kidnapping descended on the school in force. Mother was collected from the young wives and joined a crisis meeting in Miss Evans's office. I was still there and so was Mrs Lewis now looking very pathetic and nervous. Mum came in having been briefed by the police along the way. When Miss Evans joined us again she had a big policeman with her who was obviously taking charge. He sat himself down in Miss Evans's chair behind Miss Evans's desk and looked at each one of us in turn before speaking.

"My name is Detective Chief Inspector Benton and I will be heading the investigation." He turned to my mother. "Let me assure you Mrs Albon that no effort will be spared to find your son and, God willing, when we do he will be safe and well."

I don't think that my mother started to cry but I do remember she didn't speak as she reached out and took my hand. It made me feel silly and just like a baby. When you are eight years old you do not want your mother to hold your hand do you ?

The policeman continued. "I've got twenty-five men searching outwards from the school and Miss Evans has given me all the essential facts for the moment. Now what I need next is a recent picture of David."

"We can help there," Miss Evans spoke. "We've just has school photographs taken and we've kept a copy of every child's picture for our records. Mrs Lewis could you please go and find the copy of David Albon's photograph."

"Thank you Miss Evans. Now I've got three loudspeaker vans on their way over and when they are here they'll start touring the streets. The press have been informed and an appeal as to his whereabouts will be in all the evening papers."

The phone rang and was quickly answered by Miss Evans. The police may have taken over everything else but it was still her office even if she could not sit in her chair at her desk. Up went the hand and any speaking she did was via the corner of her mouth. She spoke just a few words before addressing all.

"That was David's father, he's on his way from work."

I did not believe anything could possibly have happened to Di. Who would ever want to kidnap him ? I was sure he must have done something stupid and would very soon turn up. Newspapers, police, loudspeaker vans, there would be hell to pay when they did find him. All that trouble and who was going to pay for it all ?

A special assembly was called for the whole school to help the police find out exactly who had seen him last. Stupid Brother Di, Di Central Eating with the single tooth, what was he up to ?

The remainder of the morning came and went, very soon it was lunch time. Miss Evans offered my mother a school dinner, as if she wasn't suffering enough. Sensibly she refused but all of the police accepted demolishing huge piles of ginger stodge. When my father turned up he thought we should go home but mother refused. She wanted to stay at school and besides the police were watching the house so if Di did turn up.

I think Mum was convinced that Di was dead, it was difficult to tell what Dad was thinking but I knew the police secretly though the same as Mum. But I knew different, I knew nothing was wrong. I could sense everything was perfectly alright. Di wasn't dead, it was all a big fuss about nothing. Far away in the offices of the Evening Mail compositors were preparing the headlines. What would the neighbours say ?

The secretary brought in a letter for Miss Evans to sign. She read it through before scrawling her name at the bottom. It had not been typed on ordinary paper but on one of those old fashioned Roneo stencils ready for duplicating. It was a message to all parents explaining about Di, urging both care of their own children, warning them not to talk to strangers and at the same time appealing for help find the missing boy.

"I'll see that every child gets a copy to take home before the end of school Miss Evans."

"Thank you." Miss Evans voice was starting to sound unsteady.

We then sat for a while in silence. It could not have been for more than a few moments but it felt like an age. Mum looked at Dad and tried to force a smile. Detective Chief Inspector Benton studied the surface of Miss Evans desk and doodled on her pink blotter. Miss Evans wanted to tell him to stop but said nothing. Mrs Lewis sat twisting her hands in her lap and I shuffled my feet on the carpet.

The quiet was shattered by a fierce knock on the door. It burst open without anyone inviting the caller to enter. He stood there with his cap in his hands.

"Found him in one of the bins Missus. Must have been hiding there and fallen asleep. I'd no idea he was there until I tipped out the bins and he tumbled out into one of the troughs. Fair gave the old boar a fright I can tell you. 'Fraid he's in a bit of a mess but seems to be OK otherwise. Sorry about that Missus."

Bit of a mess ? Bit of a mess ? He stank ! Covered in head to foot in the past two days' school dinners he smelt like a decomposing compost heap. Mum started to cry and hugged him to her getting the filth all over her Young Wives Club best dress.

All my Dad could say was, "Better get you home and into the bath."

Miss Evans managed a smile even though Di was dripping all kinds of horrible stuff over her carpet. The secretary had to go round and collect in all of the letters she had given to the children. The police packed up and went away as quickly as they had come, sorry they didn't have a juicy kidnap or murder to get their teeth into.

Talking of teeth, when the paperboy dropped The Evening Mail through our letter box that day there was Brother Di's toothless grin beaming out from the front page. What an idiot ! Hiding in a pig bin ! I swear the stink stayed with him for a week. Above the picture ran the headline:

The Wild Adventure Of Di Central Eating

I guess with the space reserved for a report of a missing child they had to fill it with something. Mum cut out the article and David, to the best of my knowledge, still has it. The Wild Adventure Of Di Central Eating !

Something from Beppo: You have remembered that letter haven't you ? T ? I hope so. Don't forget it, I need you to add a second letter – Y. Why ? No, not *why* but Y. Two letters to remember: T and Y ? Why ? Don't ask me why, all will be revealed in good time. On the subject of time, it is now time for Di to Go fishing.

DI'S FIRST FISH:

I can't honestly remember when or why I took up the sport of fishing, a more unlikely pastime I cannot imagine There is nothing in this world today that would induce me to crouch at some water's edge on a damp Saturday morning, a maggot impaled on a hook at the end of a length of nylon line hoping beyond hope that some gullible fish would entangle its mouth on my lure. But at the age of nine I obviously thought differently.

Nearly every Saturday morning between the months of June and the following March I could be seen at my favourite spot on the bank of Powel's Pool casting my float after fish. (April and May were months of agony being the closed season for coarse fishing when any trip to the water's edge would have been highly illegal.)

Powel's Pool was a small lake a few miles away from my home and well stocked with perch, chub, roach and dace. It was even said there was the odd pike or two lurking in the depths but they were too cunning for the likes of a nine year old school boys. There was one spot in particular I favoured on the lake, a series of three steps that led down to the water. I have no idea why they were there, they were far too small to be use to launch a sailing boat, but they were idea for our needs.

I had a fine collection of fishing tackle the pride of which was my rod. This was a ten foot split cane model that had once belonged to my grandfather. I never knew him as he died when my own father was a small child, having contracted tuberculosis in the trenches of World War One. My grandmother found the rod in the loft of her house and I was so please when she gave it to me. There was just one problem. It had been a three piece rod and she could only find the bottom two sections. Not to be put off I replaced it with one of my Dad's bamboo tomato sticks to which I carefully fastened two rings fashioned out of paper clips, bent into circles round a pencil. It worked well enough and landed many an unsuspecting tiddler.

Not that actually catching the fish was all that important. It was the bike ride to the lake, meeting up with friends, showing off one's fishing tackle collection, munching cheese sandwiches with a hand that had only moments before been plunged into a tin of crawling maggots that made up the expedition. Any catch was only secondary, a bonus if you like.

For most of these expeditions my companion was a lad who rejoiced in the name of Tubby-Taylor. Poor kid wasn't even fat but there were two boys in our gang of friends with the surname of Taylor. Something had to be done to make it clear which one you were talking about so one became known as Tubby-Taylor, I don't think he minded very much.

Now, many years later, I can feel a small satisfaction realising how important it was for Di to emulate his brother but when I was nine it was nothing more than a confounded nuisance. Week after week , Saturday after Saturday, he begged me to take him along. He tried to bribe me , he tried to get my mother to force me to take him along and he tried to appeal to my slender better nature but all without success. For most of the season of 1962 I managed to fend him off but then things took a fatal turn.

For Christmas Great Aunt Gladys brought him a fishing rod. Whatever possessed her to do that I can not imagine. She was a lovely lady, I cared for her deeply, and I had done her no wrong. So why did I merit such a punishment ? Nevertheless there it was on Christmas morning, a two-piece junior anglers rod complete with reel, line, float and a packet of hooks. It would have been mean then, I guess, to refuse him so I reluctantly gave in. I wish now that I hadn't.

First of all Mum wouldn't allow Di to ride his bike to Powel's Pool so Dad had to take us in the car. True enough he didn't shop with us, returning to pick us up four hours later, but who ever heard of going fishing by having a lift in a car ? Tubby-Taylor was good about it and said nothing as we clambered out of Dad's Austin Cambridge. That was a car and a half. It had white walled tyres and a flash of white paint down each side. With a top speed of ninety miles an hour it was a beastie of a motor car. Unfortunately Dad wrote it off in a collision with a Vauxhall Vellox and replaced it with a more sedate Austin Traveller. But never mind about that.

Enough about cars, back to fishing. I has been lectured for an age by Mum about what I was and what I was not allowed to let Di do. As if he would ever take any notice of me. It was him that needed telling, not me. We were only to be away for a few hours and usually I had to make do with two rounds of cheese sandwiches but the day Di came along Mum sent us with enough to feed an army. As well as double the amount of sandwiches there was a flask of soup, packets of crisps, chocolate biscuits and a big bag of apples. If we had stopped to eat it all there would never have been any time to fish.

We ground the crisps and mixed the resulting crumble with lumps of bread which we then tossed into the lake for ground bait. Perhaps that was what caused it to happen, I don't know, but if it was then Smiths could have patented the idea and made a fortune out of the alternative use for their crisps.

As I recall, Tubby-Taylor was very kind to Di. He didn't have any brothers and sisters of his own to make a fuss of, wishing he wasn't an only child. Lucky kid, he didn't know he was born, I'd have given him my brother any day of the week. He helped Di unpack his junior angler's kit and put the rod together. It was a two-piece metal affair with a plastic handle and plastic rod rings.

The reel, also made of plastic, was a centre pin effort fixed to the rod by stout rubber bands. There could not have been more than a couple of dozen yards of line but the breaking strain was at least twenty-pounds. Goodness knows what the makers expected anyone to catch.

Di carefully selected two fat juicy maggots, pinched them between his fingers then plunged the hook into them. I was never all that keen myself on putting maggots on hooks, always settling for a quick stab and getting it over with. Di, however, took his time and threaded the hook down the bodies until it was totally disguised.

It took four casts before Di successfully landed the maggots in the right part of the lake. Four casts each with Tubby-Taylor standing behind him issuing careful instructions and advice. Casts one and two landed no more than a few feet from the bank with a dull plop into water too shallow even for a minnow. Number three went in the opposite direction landing some twenty feet behind us in the field. But number four was perfect, at least so Tubby-Taylor said. Di looked pleased with himself, his ear to ear grin about his face. Whatever did he think he was going to catch with such a pathetic set up ? Junior angler's kit my left foot !

Thinking back now, some thirty or more years after the event, I don't think I was qualified to make such a comment. I was not, after all, myself the world's greatest fisherman, far from it. Tubby-Taylor. On the other hand, was quite a fair angler seldom failing to fill his keep net but, somehow, I was never so lucky. The fish liked the bait well enough but always managed to nibble the maggot off the hook without snaring itself on the barb.

For that reason on the day Di came along I decided to use a spinner and try for one of the legendary pike in the deep waters of the lake. On the very rare occasions anyone caught one they always had their picture in the local newspaper and I quite fancied having it stuffed and mounted in a case on my bedroom wall.

I had a fixed spool reel and with the weight of a heavy spinner I was able to cast a long way into the lake. I guess I was showing of in front of Di; casting out, reeling in and casting out again. I know I didn't have much hope of bagging a pike but that didn't matter, Di didn't have the slightest chance of bagging anything ! Then it happened.

The squeal was almost deafening. "My float's gone under the water. Look !"

"Strike !" Tubby called, leaving his own rod and moving to stand behind Di.

"Pull the rod up sharply to fix the hook in its mouth. Here, let me show you."

He needn't have bothered for the fish was already firmly on the end and taking like from the reel. "Start to wind him in. Nice and slowly, nice and gently. Keep the line tight so he doesn't tangle but don't rush him just in case you snap the line."

Snap the line ? What did Tubby-Taylor think Di had caught ? A whale ! That line was strong enough to land a pike ! A pike ? Oh no he couldn't have, not a pike. The humiliation. Please not a pike. I wound my line in and stood to watch, my fingers secretly crossed against it being a pike. At least that is why I think I had them crossed. Deep down it may be I was just a little pleased for Di. After all he was my brother and I did care for him even if he was a champion prat.

I need not have worried too much, it wasn't a pike. There was no way Di could have managed to reel in a pike on his own using a plastic centre pin reel. The fish was offering very little resistance, as if it knew its fate. Either that or it was a geriatric of the aquatic world. No doubt it had been through all this many, many times before. The tempting breakfast that turned out to have a hook in it, that hook pushing through its lip, the indignity of being pulled by the mouth through water then up into the air before being disentangled and placed in the prison of a keep net. A couple of hours swimming round and round trying to find a way out of the net until up ended and freed back into the lake. You would think it would have learned from past experiences wouldn't you ?

Perhaps that was why my own catch was always so modest. All the fish in Powel's Pool had been through it before and knew what they must do to avoid at all costs maggots suspended in the water. Perhaps their mothers warned them against it like ours did telling us not to take sweets from strange men. Or perhaps the drowning maggots could communicate with the fish warning, "It's a trap, please don't eat me."

For a short cast it was taking a lot of turns on that plastic reel to pull the fish in but it wasn't fighting and so Di was coping well on his own. Although Tubby-Taylor was there with lots of advice he did not actually have to take a hand himself, safely leaving all the work to Di.

I caught sight of Di's catch as it was pulled through the water. It wasn't a pike. Relief. But then I found myself urging Di on, willing him to land it. Too often I had lost fish myself in the last moments. If the fish was not firmly on the hook it was all too easy for it to escape when the line was slackened as you reached down with your hand to lift it out. If this particular fish knew that dodge it would be the end of the world. If it got away Di would be upset, I would have been mortified. Brother Di was the absolute pest of a little brother but my brother he was and right then I was sharing his pride.

Tubby-Taylor knew the dodge well and was at the water's edge to lift the catch clear and render escape impossible. In a glitter the silver of it came clear of the surface. I need not have worried for this fish knew neither this nor any other dodge. It was a novice and this was its first time.

I don't know if fish have emotions or understand fear. I expect a marine biologist would say not but this fish did. Looking down I could see the fear in its eyes. It looked wildly about itself unable to move anything but its eyes as Tubby-Taylor held it firmly in his right hand. That poor creature was absolutely terrified and I felt sorry for it.

Tubby showed Di how to unfix the hook from its mouth. "Do you want to hold him ?" He asked.

It was a perch. It was about six ounces and five inches long. It wasn't very old, perhaps in its first season and no doubt then thinking that its short life was over. Di stroked it with the back of his forefinger.

"If you want to hold it wet your hands first, a dry human hand is like a red hot poker to a fish. Watch its spikes," Tubby explained, "the can be quite sharp and will stick in you. See how I've got them folded back."

Di nodded.

Suddenly it felt all wrong that it was Tubby-Taylor coaching Di and not me his older brother but what could I do ? "That's a fine fish Di," I said by way of slight compensation.

"Take him and put him in the keep net." Tubby continued. "Gently, that's the way."

Di did as he was instructed.

"I reckon it was that special mix of ground bait we put together," I added. "Think we'd better put some up for next Saturday ?"

Neither Tubby-Taylor nor I caught anything that day, nor for that matter did we the following week. Shortly before it was time for Dad to pick us up we let Di's fish go, free to swim and free to fight another day.

Di never went fishing again and I stopped later that season. Tubby-Taylor moved away when his dad got a new job and somehow it wasn't the same fishing alone. I suppose I could have gone with Di but in one day he had become the expert and I the novice. In a strange way it kind of drew us closer together. The way Tubby had acted towards him made me jealous, he being the big brother that I should have been, the big brother Di expected me to be.

When we got home Di was strangely modest about his victory. Once he had shared a few basic facts with Mum and Dad he never spoke again about the expedition, the catching of his first and his last fish.

Something more from Beppo: Is your memory functioning OK ? Have you remembered the letter OK ? No not O and K but T and Y. I hope so because you are now to add the letter P to your brain cells, P as in Platinum, Plated and Pitchforks.

PLATINUM PLATED PITCHFORKS:
Brother Di was nothing if he was not gullible, you could get him to almost believe anything. He still believed in the tooth fairy until he was fourteen and as far as I am aware he still writes to Father Christmas every year. It was on a family holiday that I

decided to put this credibility to test, to see just how naïve he was, to measure for posterity his innocence.

Every year my father world organise a summer holiday for the family. For two years we went to Weston-Super-Mare in Somerset, another time we went to Blackpool and on another we went to Bridlington. I remember it rained every day we were at Bridlington. Today when people jet off for Disneyland in Florida or the beaches of the Mediterranean, Bridlington, Blackpool and Weston-Super-Mare sound very dull places but as kids we looked forward to our visits for weeks, if not months, ahead longing for the adventures they held in store.

It was usual for us to rent a caravan and for Mum to do all the cooking just as she did at home. It hardly could have been much of a holiday for her but she would have it no other way. She always, as well, imagined there would be no shops where we were staying and that her family would devour twice, if not three times, their usual diet while in the fresh air. She, therefore, packed the boot of the car with box after box of provisions. So much so that there was never enough room for the suitcases. These then had to ride on the roof of the car secured to a luggage rack by yards of jute rope. She also insisted we took almost every stitch of clothing we owned just in case. After all you could never trust the British weather.

For this particular holiday Dad decided on something totally different and much more ambitious. No, it wasn't a cruise down the Nile, at nine years of age I did not know where the Nile was, but the next best thing. For a period of seven days Dad had rented a houseboat on the Shropshire Union Canal. We were to drive up the A5 to the Welsh town of Llangollen where the boat was moored. We would then work our way eastward towards Shropshire. It sounded terrific.

Llangollen rests in a valley through which pass the A5 and the A539 trunk roads, the track of the Shrewsbury Bala, the River Dee and the Shropshire union Canal. Of course I did not know all that then, it's very easy to set it down now with a copy of the ordnance survey map by my side as I write. What I did know was that on the canal sat our home for the next week.

Dad had a photograph of her. She was called the *Penowern* but we had no idea what that meant. I tried to find out as I put these notes together but have been unable to discover any reference anywhere to the name. I suspect it to be of Welsh origin but as I have said before my family is not Welsh and so it remains a mystery.

Penowern, bless her rotting hull, was hardly a Nile cruiser. Built at the same time Noah was taking sailing lessons, she was not a cruiser even of the Shropshire Union Canal. I think *stig* is the word I am looking for but never mind it was our passport to adventure and it would suit my purpose with Di very well. Very well indeed.

On the first night as we lay in bed I set the seeds. We boys were sleeping in the forward cabin while Mum and Dad were in the rear. Cabin ? More like a cupboard really but there you are.

"Di are you awake ?" It was a silly question. I'd have known well enough if he was asleep for he snored like a pig. It was something to do with his sleeping on his back and having no teeth in his mouth.

"Yeh."

"Do you know what a leprechaun is ?"

"No."

"Well do you know what a gnome is ?"

"Next door has one sitting by the side of their fish pond."

What a fool ! If anyone was at the back of the queue when the Good Lord dished out brains then it was Brother Di. "That's just a model stupid. I mean the real thing."

"What is the real thing then ?"

"Every country's got them you know, little people I mean. In Ireland they call them leprechauns and in England they're called gnomes."

"Get off."

I ignored this and continued. "In Denmark they're known as trolls. I don't remember what they are called in France."

"Frogs ?"

Oh the wit, the humour not bad I suppose for a ten year old but however did I cope ?

"In Wales I think they are called Morons."

"I don't believe you. How would you know anyway ?"

"You learn about these things when you get older. We did it in school but of you are too young to understand."

"I'm nearly seven now," he defended.

"I guess you are so perhaps it's about time you started to learn. After all we are in Wales and you never know."

There my explanation was brought to a sudden and rapid halt. With spot on timing Mum came in and gave us a fearful ear bashing for still being awake. As kids she never hit us but she could kill you stone dead at fifty paces with one lash of her tongue. You never went back for second helpings of that I can tell you. Silent we were then until breakfast but I had said all that needed to be said for the time being. The gem of an idea had been set and Di could sleep on it. The next stage of my plan I had already put into action.

Day two of the holiday saw us pull up the moorings, Dad cranked up Penowern's aging engine and spluttered out of Llangollen. It was a warm sunny day, Dad was at the wheel, Mum was in the kitchen, sorry I mean galley, while Di and I were sitting on deck trailing sticks in the water. I knew it would come, his curiosity would demand it, so I tried to be patient and just waited.

"Richard."

"Yes."

"What's this, do you know ?"

Perfect !

"Where did you get that from ?" I tried to sound excited.

"Found it in my pocket this morning."

"Go on, you never."

"Yes I did."

"You lucky kid. In your pocket ?"

"Yes. Do you know what it is ?"

"Course I do."

"What is it then ?"

"It's a platinum plated pitchfork." How's that for alliteration ? Not bad in a nine year old. "Must have been left by a Moron."

"What's a Moron ?"

I wanted to say "You are" but resisted and instead, "Like I was telling you last night."

"Gnomes and all that stuff ?"

"That's it, you've got it in one !"

Before we left home I had carefully made a number of these so called platinum plated pitchforks. I had taken small twigs, striped the bark and wrapped silver paper round them. It was unlikely they would have fooled a geriatric blind man with a wooden leg but even such a person was infinitely higher on the intelligence scale than my Bother Di.

"What would a Moron want this for ?"

"Di, I really am not sure you are old enough to know yet."

For a small child I was showing patience not typical of my age. I got up and walked back to where Dad was wrestling with the wheel. Penowern had something of a mind of its own. Although general progress was being made in a forward direction it was not in a straight line but weaving one elongated s-shape after another. I'm not sure if it was Dad who couldn't control it or if the rudder was not connected to the wheel, but our voyage was beginning to attract attention from other boat users. Some just laughed, others waved fists and some swore the most terrible oaths. I think Dad was beginning to wish we had gone back to Bridlington even if it did rain there all the time.

Behind us the engine chugged away with an irregular beat, well not a beat actually, more of a thump and a clang. It was so clapped out it was a wonder it turned over at all. Every few minutes it would cough, splutter, falter and recover.

"What's up with the engine Dad ?"

"You tell me. It's full of gremlins, that's all I know."

"What's a gremlin Dad ?" Di had joined us back on the bridge.

"Little men that crawl into machinery and cause sabotage."

"Nice one Dad ! I couldn't have put it better myself. I looked Di in the eye and nodded back to the front of the boat. He got then message.

Safely seated back at the bow, again trailing sticks in the water, I made my next move.

"Wouldn't mention that pitchfork to Dad if I were you."

"Why not ?"

"I keep telling you, you'll have to wait until you are older. Then you'll understand."

"But I'm nearly seven," he protested again.

"So you've told me many times before." I feigned a certain hesitation before continuing, "OK but you must promise to listen carefully."

"I promise."

"Morons," I explained are the little Welsh people. You don't often see them as they're very shy and only come out at night. They live in small tribes along the banks of rivers and canals. Dad calls them gremlins but morons, gremlins they're all the same thing."

"What do they do ?"

"They steal food."

"And sabotage boat engines ?" Di interrupted.

"Rather looks that way doesn't it. You heard yourself Dad say they've been in this boat engine."

"Have they come onboard to nick Mum's cooking then ?"

"Could be." That was an idea to work on.

Di pulled my pitchfork out of his pocket. "What do they use these for ?"

"When they sabotage and break things they use their platinum plated pitchforks by sticking them into whatever it is."

"Cor. They're trying to sabotage my trousers then ?"

Di was hooked, convinced that little men with the unlikely name of Morons were swarming all over Wales once it became dark creating mischief with their platinum plated pitchforks. I told you he was gullible didn't I ? I'd get him.

Shortly after lunch we reached our first lock. What a palaver that turned out to be. First of all the lock gates were closed against us, with the lock water at a higher level, so we had to draw it off before Penowern could be driven in. Dad opened the sluice gates but forgot to close those at the other end. The result was the level in the lock remained the same while all the water did was to flow in at one end and out at the other. By the time anyone realised there were four other boats lined up behind us waiting to use the lock.

Then Penowern refused to approach the lock in a straight line, hitting first one lock gate and then bouncing onto the other. Fierce shouts came from Mum as plates crashed to the floor in the kitchen, or do I mean galley, where she was trying to do the washing up. The gates were quickly closed and the troublesome Penowern captured. The water rose and the folk from the now five boats queuing behind us dashed to open the forward lock gates in order to speed us on our way.

Di and I thought it may perhaps be a good idea to walk along the tow path rather than entrust our lives to Penowern. The only problem was we had to keep stopping in order to let the old tub catch us up. Ambling along I put my hand into my pocket and produced two more platinum plated pitchforks.

"Where did you get those from ?" Di enquired excitedly.

"Found them just before lunch."

"Where ?"

"One by the engine, remember how Dad said there were Gremlins in it, and the other was in the sugar bowl."

"Cor !" The current expression in use today I think is gob-smacked.

"I told you they stole food didn't I ? Well it looks like these Welsh Morons have been nicking Mum's sugar."

"She'll kill 'em if ever she find out."

"Don't tell her then."

Although Mum and Dad had been bang on cue, almost as if I had briefed them. I hadn't honest, I did not want Di saying anything to them and blowing my plan. On a count of ten Di had reached seven on the gullible scale and was still climbing. I fully intended him to reach ten and the jackpot before the end of the holiday.

Penowern's progress along the Shropshire Union Canal continued to be slow. There were two more locks that day that had to be navigated, each one every bit as bad as the first we had encountered. Although Dad claimed to have mastered the tiller she still wove her way forward like a snake, defying all attempts towards a straight line. The engine sounded like nails being poured into a tin can while a hippopotamus belched through an out of tune mouth organ. I doubt if we managed ten miles all day long.

In the late afternoon we moored up and Mum served dinner. My mum was, and still is, a fantastic cook. In spite of all the adversity she managed a three course meal as if it had been served in a top restaurant. If the Morons had been about they never touched that meal. Enjoying each mouthful we tried to put out of mind the difficulties of the day. Then Dad brought us sharply back to reality.

I very much doubt if I knew then what an aqueduct was and am certain Di hadn't a clue but I dare not speak. I didn't want Di to get on to the subject of gremlins and morons, at least not in front of Mum and Dad. I put a finger to my lips and indicated for him to keep quiet.

We moored at that spot for two nights and did not reach the aqueduct until the day after. It marked the turning pint of the holiday, the point that is where we turned Penowern round and headed back to Llangollen. Let me explain.

The day after Mum's gastronomic extravaganza none of us got up very early. It was food again that woke Di and I. Somehow it is quite impossible to sleep through the small of bacon cooking. We stuffed ourselves then made ready for the assault on the aqueduct. Mum insisted all the washing was safely done before we cast off, she had not forgotten the previous day when we entered, or at least tried to enter, our first lock. Goodness knew what an aqueduct would be able to do !

Once the last plate had been dried and put away Dad went to start the engine. The starter whirred and the engine spluttered but refused to fire. Dad tried a second, a third and then a fourth time but it just didn't want to know. A check of the fuel tank and lines showed all to be well. Another try, still no good. Next check the electrics, they seemed to be OK. The engine was on strike !

It took Dad two hours to strip it down, clean everything and put it all back together again. "Should be fine now," he assured but we simply did not share his confidence I am afraid.

Another turn of the key. The buz of the starter but again nothing more. Out came the tools and everything was stripped down for a second time. Hands were scrubbed, lunch eaten and yet another attempt made. By then Dad was decidedly rattled. This was not the way things had been planned. Next year we would all go back to Bridlington !

"I can't understand it," he muttered. "I've been over everything twice now. This engine's certainly got gremlins in it."

"Gremlins ?"

"Gremlins Di or what is it you called them ?"

"Morons Dad but they can't be stopping the engine now."

Damn it he was going to let it all out and I couldn't shut him up. He had his back to me and the way he was talking to Dad it was impossible to get between them.

"Why not ?" I think Dad was desperate and willing to take advice even from a six year old. But he was not as desperate as I was and still I could not catch Di's eye.

"Because I fed them Dad, they won't break the engine because I fed them and now they'll be happy."

"Fed them ? How have you fed them ?"

"I put sugar in the petrol tank Dad."

Something AGAIN from Beppo: Now for the last letter In need you top remember, don't worry you wont need any more memory after letter number four. And that letter is O, O as in orbit which was what Yuri Gagarin did around Earth That was before his sat nav messed up and he landed on Mars. Letter number four is O.

PATHFINDERS IN SPACE:

When we were kids we stood at the dawn of the space age, little did we know that with the end of the Apollo Programme there would be an about turn and man's exploration of the universe would be no nearer than it had been at the time of the cavemen. But things had once been different. Yuri Gagarin was an international hero, President Kennedy declared the United States would land a man on the moon before the end of the decade and our television screens were filled with constant speculation of space travel.

There were dozens of different programmes: Dan Dare and Flash Gordon, revamped from the generation of our parents. H G Wells First Man In The Moon from two generations even earlier, Doctor Who and one I remember in particular, Pathfinders In Space.   This told of a family who were accidentally blasted into outer space visiting the Moon, Mars and Venus before making their way home again. Kids no longer dreamed of being train drivers but set their hearts on becoming astronauts. Things were the same for Di and me. The only difference was we had a real live space rocket in our back garden.

Project Mercury was all about putting manned American space craft in Earth orbit. Kids stuff, I had my own eyes set deeper into space. I had a chart on my bedroom wall diagrammatically showing all the planets of the solar system orbiting the Sun. Mercury, Venus, Earth, Mars, Jupiter, Saturn, Uranus, Neptune, Pluto. I knew them all, how many moons each had, how long it took to rotate about its own axis and how long it took to orbit about the Sun. Not that I needed it but there was a little saying to help you remember the order in which they came: *Men Very Easily Make Jugs Serving Useful Numerous Purposes.*

I taught this to Di explaining which planets we would visit in our homemade space rocket. First we would go to Mars, we wouldn't bother with the Moon, and then to Venus where I was convinced we would find life. Venusian little green men which we would tame and bring home to Earth. To a nine year old it was harmless play, make believe, but Di I am afraid took it as gospel.

Our very own space ship was constructed one Saturday morning. First of all I had taken myself down to our local greengrocer and scrounged from its grumpy proprietor, Mr Tom O'Connell, eight of the wooden boxes he had his oranges delivered in. That in itself was a major undertaking, perhaps easier than flying to Mars. O'Connell would only burn the boxes but protest beyond reason about the small boys that tried to beg them to make go-kart trollies not to mention space rockets. Sometimes he charged sixpence a box but would never have dared to charge me, he valued my Mother's custom in his shop far too much for that.

It took Di and I four journeys to and from O'Connell's shop in order to shift the boxes home. Although we lived just round the corner It took over half an hour to complete the task. On the last visit we called into one of the other shops in the small row that made up the local centre, Ken Riley Hardware, where we paid one shilling and nine pence to buy one pound of inch and a half round head nails. Hammer, saw, pliers and screwdriver were secretly borrowed from Dad's tool box and we were set.

We cut the boxes up into planks and then reassembled them into a square, nailing them precariously together using Dad's hammer and the nails we had brought earlier. The description *square* would be generous, rectangle an exaggeration but the four corners did at least add up to three hundred and sixty degrees. The box was big enough for Di and I to sit in and we entered by way of a small trap door constructed in the side. It had a floor but no roof and less like a space rocket it could never have been. It was my idea how to finish off the exterior and make it perfect.

I went to the garden shed and hunted out Di's wigwam tent. He used to use it when he played cowboys and indians, it was the perfect shape for a nose cone and just fitted on top of the box. I nailed the bamboo poles and the fabric sides in place. The exterior of the first inter-planetary manned space craft to leave the Earth was complete.

During the afternoon our attentions were turned to the inside. The priority was the floor. As it was, if we attempted to sit down we would very soon have had perforated bottoms from the protruding nails. Mum came up with the answer in an old carpet which when spread over the base covered safely most of the sharp bits. My Meccano construction set was employed building the life support system, propulsion unit and navigation control, the collection of wheels, levers and dials nailed to the orange box walls. It was a hard sacrifice to make but I took down the chart from my bedroom and pinned it up inside the space craft.

We needed supplies, the journey to Mars and Venus would take many days. Di had a packet of Smarties to which I added half a Mars Bar and a packet of custard cream biscuits. Our space suits comprised wellington boots and a pair of swimming goggles. I had an old camera I had paid a shilling for at the school jumble sale, that would be good for taking photographs of any aliens we met.

"We've forgotten something," Di said.

"What ?" I looked round at our collection, it all looked perfectly in order to me.

"A toilet," he explained. "We'll never make it all the way to Venus without needing a wee."

He had a point of course and I wondered what real spacemen did. I suppose those orbiting the Earth were only up there for a few hours but what if they got caught short ? Would Yuri Gagarin have been quite such an international hero if he'd come back with wet pants ? Then it came to me, obvious when you think about it.

"When you are weightless in space Di you don't need the toilet. Your digestion doesn't work the same so it all stays inside you."

"Oh, I see."

Better keep the drinks down though just in case.

Dad came to admire the rocket, full of sarcasm was my Dad. He stood there rubbing his chin. It frightens me now to try and imagine what he was thinking.

"We're off to Mars," Di explained.

"Are you ? Will you be gone before then lawn needs mowing or should I cut round you, difficult with it sitting here on the grass."

"No problem Dad, we've got our first test flight in the morning."

"Good. Be sure to let me know what time you decide to leave, I wouldn't want to miss the take off."

"Have you got any old paint Dad ?" I asked. "The outside looks a bit wrong as it is."

Dad found us two tins, one of green and one of pink. Hardly inter-planetary colours but we spent the rest of the afternoon applying them to Mr O'Connell's orange boxes. With care we lettered *Venusian Expedition* on one of the sides. Dad took a photograph of our efforts and years later I was embarrassed to discover we had spelt it *Venushian Expedishon.* It didn't matter at the time and was much better than having *Outspan* on the sides !

I have made mention of it before but I feel I must stress again that for me it was all a game, a childhood fantast, perfectly harmless, but to Di it was an authentic rocket that would actually fly. Perhaps at the tender age of six it didn't matter.

It had been a warm day and the forecast was mild for the night. We didn't have to go to school the next morning, being Sunday, and it was at tea Mum made the suggestion. I remember we had sardines on toast, small fish that came in flat tins opened with a key that wound a strip of metal off the side to release the lid and expose the head and tailless little fish laying in a sea of tomato sauce. We used to mash the fish onto the toast and pick out the bones before eating. I never did fancy this very much.

"Eat up Richard, you've hardly touched your tea."

"Not very hungry Mum."

"After the work you've done all day. This is a perfect meal for a spaceman."

Funny, I'd never seen Dan Dare or Flash Gordon dining on sardines on toast. In Pathfinders in Space they ate food from tubes that looked a bit like toothpaste.

"That's a shame because I thought you and Di may like to camp out overnight in your space rocket."

Was it worth it ? I guessed it was so tucked into an ample helping of sardines on toast. Camping out in the space rocket, what a prospect, what a chance for our first test flight. My sudden liking for sardines on toast told my Mother how very keen I was on her suggestion. Di had more to say on the matter, he prattled on in excitement for an age.

"Oh Mummy can we really camp out tonight in the space rocket ?" He spoke with elation spitting bits of sardine across the room.

"Just don't disturb the neighbours," Dad added, "the way you snore some nights they'll think we are having an earthquake."

There'd be no sleeping that night, we were off into outer space. It was just possible we wouldn't even be back in time for breakfast.

Sleeping bags were unpacked from the upstairs cupboard and laid out on the floor of the space rocket. A torch was found and entrusted to me for safe keeping. Mum, conscious of her ever present concern that we should be well fed, packed a picnic supper. The way she used to feed us as kids it's a wonder we both never grew up to resemble the obese characters one sees in childrens' comics.

Eventually all was set but first there was something very important to do. Saturday evening was Pathfinders In Space on the television and the next adventure to watch. Already dressed in our pyjamas but supplemented with woollen jumpers and a pair of socks each, we sat round that old Murphy black and white television set waiting for the music that would introduce our favourite programme of the week.

That particular episode saw the explorers stranded on a Venusian landscape without water. As it built towards the climax relief came in the form of vegetation that, when broken, had water inside instead of sap.

"Better make sure we take plenty of water with us."

"No problem, Mum's put up a flask of coffee for us."

There was no problem getting us off to bed that night. By eight thirty we were safely tucked up in sleeping bags inside the rocket, the launch count down proceeding steadily. One by one I ran through the pre-launch checks: life support, booster rockets, retro thrusters and artificial gravity. Di was impatient, demanding to known when we would be on our way.

"You can't hurry things," I explained, "do you want to disintegrate a million particles as we burst through escape velocity just because we failed just because we failed to check one area of the ship ? You can't rush science Di."

At about T-minus one hour twenty I realised that Di was asleep. Too tired or too bored to wait any longer. I think I may only made it as far as T-minus fifty before I joined him in dreamland.

I don't remember what I dreamed about, that is if I dreamed at all. When I awoke the next day my mind was quite clear and empty but for a short moment I could not figure out where I was.

"Wakey-wakey my two little spacemen, breakfast is twenty minutes away."

"Morning Mum," I stirred slowly, shielding my eyes from the early sun.

If I awoke slowly Di blizzarded his way into conscience. "We're home already ! Boy, what an adventure. I didn't like Mars much did you but Venus was just super. Can we go back there tomorrow ? That Supreme Leader was frightening wasn't he ? Can you remember his name ? Wasn't that city strange ? I think I've left my goggles behind, no I haven't here they are in my sleeping bag. Please can we go back tomorrow ? Do you think

Mum will let us ? It came out in a gibberish splutter of euphoria that continued on and on and on. He was a real born again fruitcake, my brother.

He hardly came up for air during breakfast and was still confabulating at lunch time. During the afternoon we went to visit our grandmother where he churned it all out again. He honestly thought we had flown about the solar system overnight in a rocket made from a wigwam and Mr O'Connell's orange boxes. I presumed he dreamed it all. I envied him that dream, but to regard it as reality was naive even for a six year old.

Every Sunday we used to visit my grandmother, it was something of a ritual. Some weeks we were invited to stay for tea while on others we left to eat at home. The invitation was a kind of barometer measuring how the old lady felt about our company on each particular visit. With Di chattering away ten to the dozen we certainly weren't offered anything that Sunday afternoon. I don't think my gran had any interest at all in interplanetary travel.

He was still going on about it at bedtime and went to school the next day telling all who would listen about his adventure. Do you remember when you were in the infants how you used to have to stand up on a Monday morning in front of the rest of the class to tell your *news* ? No prizes for guessing what Di's news was. Mrs Lewis told Mum about it at parents' evening a few weeks later saying what a vivid imagination her son had and showing her the story he had written up in his news book: Di Central Eating – Pathfinder In Space and First Man on Venus.

Sorry about this everyone, Beppo speaking AGAIN. Sorry to have been interrupting your reading between Di's adventures but I am doing so as David told me I must !

You have remembered those four letters I hope: T – Y – P – O.

You human homosapien mankind species have some strange words in your dictionary, words we clowns would never think of allowing to fall from our mouths. *Typographical error*, what on earth does that mean ? David abbreviated it to Typo and instructed me to here offer an apology for any you have stumbled over while reading our adventures. We clowns have a word Toepin which means the way our socks are pinned to our feet but it has nothing at all to do with writing. If you ask me this typo stuff is silly ! Clowns are funny, not silly. Toepin is funny, typo is silly. Besides these are adventures for children written for grownups to read so the odd spelling mistake, aka typo, ads reality to the words. Is that OK David, tough luck if it's not. Typo, why not spell it tiepoo ? **Beppo.**

ROCK AND ROLL SUPERSTAR:
We kids grew up in a magical age the like of which had not been seen before and has not been seen since. It was a decade that began with Rock and Roll and ended with Flower Power. The austerity of the post war era was gone and all were able to look forward to a bright and exciting future. With a little bit of luck, hard work and talent anyone could be transformed from rags to riches.

Talent was a word we were all familiar with, had we not heard the parable of the talents. Talent was a coin, the wise young man in the story had been given five, or was it ten, talents and had made ten more. The fool had been given just one and he had buried it in the ground. It was confusing, therefore, when we saw a poster in the library window advertising a talent competition. Did it mean they were going to hand out talents and that we had to go out and make more before some predetermined day of judgement ? I thought to myself I wanted nothing to do with that.

Next day in school assembly the headmistress, Miss Evans, started to talk about the contest and very soon I realised it had absolutely nothing at all to do with the Biblical talents. This had something to do with singing, dancing and telling jokes. I had about as much interest in that as I did in the parable at Sunday School. I kind of stopped listening but I do remember something about local heats before a city final and the first prize being a family holiday to Butlins. Entry forms could be collected from the secretary's office during morning playtime.

Butlins, everybody wanted to go to Butlins but I was rather surprised to learn that our headmistress, the revered Miss G M Evans had never heard of Butlins Holiday Camps.

At the end of World War Two along came Billy Butlin who brought up some disused army camp, bunged in the odd swimming pool, imported a load of holiday-makers, laid on dawn to dusk complementary entertainment and becoming a multi-millionaire in the process. Every child wanted to go to Butlins but somehow it wasn't exactly our Mum and Dad's scene. Something I once remember being said included not touching it with a disinfected bargepole. Although I let most of Miss Evans assembly pass over my head I think it was the prospect of time at a holiday camp that made Di prick up his ears. After school that day he brought home an entry form.

The competition was being organised by the town council with heats in each of its local areas. The finals were to be held in the town hall with a first prize of a family holiday for four at a Butlins Holliday Camp of the winner's choice.

"Well what could you do ?" Dad asked later peering over the top of the evening paper.

"I'm going to sing."

"Can you sing ?"

"'Course I can sing, when I grow up I am going to be a rock and roll megastar."

"If Richard were to sing with you it could be a duet like the Everly Brothers." Thank you Mum I did not need any suggestions like that one.

"More like the Beverley Sisters," Dad added.

"There's three of them," Mum defended, "and I for one am proud that Di wants to enter."

"Better not win though 'cos I'm not going to Butlins." That was fine, if Di won we'd go without him.

"What are you going to sing ?"

"Wooden Heart by Elvis Presley."

Now my Mother fancied herself as something of a musician, she had piano lessons when she was a child, so took on the coaching of her son in the Banners Gate heat of the Royal Sutton Coldfield Children's Talent Contest. We had an old piano in our front room and every afternoon, after school, Di would practice while Mum plonked away on the keys. He could not have sounded less like Elvis Presley and I'm sure Elvis had never heard of the songs Di elected to sing.

It could be that was a bit unfair, somehow I do not think Di chose the songs himself but rather had them chosen for him by Mum. She turned him right off Wooden Heart and refused anything by Cliff Richard who she regarded as some here today and gone tomorrow pop artist who would never last.

Entrants in the singing section of the contest had to select two songs and very soon the house filled with those Di was to sing. You know what it is like when you can't get a tune out of your head, maddening ! Well that's how it became for us. One day I even caught Dad whistling one of them in the bathroom while shaving before work.

Mum had gone along to Curtis Music and Record Store and ordered manuscript copies of the songs. As I write now those wretched words and their accompanying melodies are starting to invade my brain again. If I can't get to sleep tonight for hearing them I'll... !

It was strange all the effort Mum was putting into preparing Di for the contest, almost as if she wanted him to win and for us all to go off to the dreaded Butlins. Even Dad was tolerant but then I guess they both knew Brother Di didn't stand a chance.

Then one week-end Dad flipped and went over the top. When he came home from work on Friday he had with him what looked like a small suitcase. When the lid was opened an old fashioned wheel to wheel tape recorder was revealed.

Such an item of equipment was a major status symbol for many families and needless to say we did not own one. At first I thought Dad had gone out and blown goodness knows how much money on it but then he explained that it was only borrowed from a friend at work. Di was about to make his first recording.

The microphone was set up on a stool by the piano, Di positioned about two feet away from it then Mum began to play. Dad was an absolute novice and there was no such thing as automatic recording levels on machines in those days. It took six attempts to get it right and even then the piano sounded hollow and distant while Di's voice was too full of treble pipes and tinny. But never mind, the recording was made although none of us had any use for it beyond that week-end, after all we did not have a tape records of our own to listen to it on.

As time for the contest drew nearer Mum took Di down to the Co-op and brought him a special outfit to wear. Blue trousers, a red checked shirt and a yellow bow tie. He looked a right idiot I can tell you and I was glad I wouldn't have to watch him perform but I'd hot that wrong. We were all going, no choice in the matter. Mum had got tickets for us all and for Gran and for Great-Aunt Gladys as well. How totally embarrassing !

The preliminary heat was not to be in the town hall but at the local secondary school. We arrived early in order to get seats near the front. Dad went and brought programmes for us all. There was Di's name together with the titles of the two songs he would be singing. He wasn't in the least bit nervous and didn't seem to realise what he was letting himself in for.

The first contestants were dreadful, a brother and sister duet. The brother played the violin and the girl a recorder. Neither were in tune and the relief on their faces when the end came was pathetic to see. The next entry was an older boy who tried to impersonate Arthur Askey. His opening line of *Hello Playmates* was the funniest thing he said during his entire act. At the end the audience politely clapped.

Di was next. Full of confidence he swaggered up onto the platform, pulled himself up to his full three feet six and a half inches then smiled. That brought a titter from one corner of the hall and I pushed myself down into my chair hoping no one would realise he was my brother.

The pianist struck up the chords of the introduction, Di drew breath then launched into his first song:

"All I want for Christmas is me two front teeth, me two front teeth, yes me two front teeth."

"All I want for Christmas is me two front teeth, yes me two front teeth, so I can wish you Merry Christmas."

Even though Christmas was still several months away there were roars of laughter from everyone in the hall, great guffaws of belly-rocking hilarity. Great-Aunt Gladys had to open her bag, take out a handkerchief and wipe away a tear. When Di had finished he took a step forward and bowed. The applause was deafening what with clapping, cheers and even the odd whistle. It went on so long he couldn't begin his second song.

When eventually silence descended Di's timing was again perfect, Mum had trained him well. He put his hands deep into his pockets, pulled out two brushes, held them up then grinned his toothless grin. Again the audience erupted and again he had to wait for quiet.

"You're a pink toothbrush, I'm a blue toothbrush will you marry me some day ?"

There were another seven contestants but none stood any chance. Di was the obvious winner. When the judges confirmed it he had go on stage again for an encore. That family holiday at Butlins was ours for the taking. After such a performance the finals in the town hall would be a walk over.

We were all very proud of Di, even I have to confess that, and I think Dad had forgotten all about his fear of Butlins Holiday Camps. On the way home we had fish and chips with a portion of scraps, all those crunchy bits of batter skimmed off the top of the fryer. Lovely.

Di had to wait four months until the finals. During that time the practices with Mum continued and confidence grew. Victory was certain. Not only did Gran and Great-Aunt Gladys come along again but when we took our seats we saw both Miss Evans and Di's teacher Mrs Lewis on the other side of the hall. So many people.

So many people to watch a victory. So many people to watch a victory that never happened. Di wasn't even placed in the top three. This time there were no wild cheers or shouts of *more – more,* just affable clapping. The first place and the holiday at Butlins went to a girl with pigtails and a brace who played the flute. How could anyone play the flute wearing a gum brace ? What had gone wrong ? You see there were four months, seventeen long weeks, between Di's victory in the heats and his singing again in the finals. Four months during which Di's teeth grown and filled the front of his mouth. Without a toothless smile *All I want for Christmas is my two front teeth* just was not funny. Poor old Di, no longer Central Eating.

Beppo again ! Something before you read the next adventure. *Please pick up any tiepoo and place it in the bins provided.* Excuse me it is spelt toepin, tiepoo is a typo !

NIPPER:
It seemed to me that Di had been nearly seven for years. If anyone asked him how old he was he would never say "Six" but always "Nearly seven". When it became apparent that he would actually make it to his seventh birthday and that it was only a couple of weeks away Mum, Dad and I put our minds together to decide what to buy for him. Mum suggested he should read more and that we could give him a set of books. Not a good idea. Offering Di a book would have been like serving bacon sandwiches to the Rabbi at a Bar-Mitzvah.

Let me digress for a brief moment and talk a little about this reading business. Although we decided not to buy Di a book for his birthday it does tie up with what we did finally get him. When I first started to learn to read and write in the infant department of Banners gate County Primary School I began with a little reader called *Nip and Fluff.* Nip was a dog and Fluff was a cat. The book told in the simplest words of their adventures. I can remember almost every word.

Here is Nip.
Here is Fluff.
Nip is a dog.
Fluff is a cat.
Nip and Fluff are playing.
Nip and Fluff are playing in the garden.

And so it went on. One short sentence on each page with a line drawing to demonstrate whatever the canine/feline duo were up to. Goodness who thought up such gibberish but countless thousands of copies were sold ensuring his fortune. Mum bought one of those copies making me read from it to her every night. When it came time for Di to start school Nip and Fluff were waiting for him and the whole process started over again.

Well enough of that, back to the plan for Di's seventh birthday. The most popular toy in the shops at that time was a Dan Dare Radio Station, a pretend toy transmitter-receiver, but it was priced at over five pounds which was well beyond Dad's intended budget. So that idea was relegated to join Mum's collection of books. Di wasn't really old enough for a train set and he used my Meccano set so they were both out as well. With three days left to go still no decision had been made. With so little time left Dad came up with the perfect idea but it was one that would involve us all far beyond Di's seventh birthday.

Looking back I am more than pleased with the decision we all came to that evening as we plotted away while Di was asleep in bed. I wonder, however, if we honestly knew what we were up to. I say *we* to include Mum, Dad and myself but I should explain I was only a very junior partner and doubt if my vote counted for all that much, if anything at all. Now that was unfair seeing how much future responsibility was to fall upon me.

Di's seventh birthday present wasn't just for him, it was kind of for all of us. Dad picked it up the day before, hiding it in Gran's house overnight. He left well before breakfast to collect it in time for Di getting out of bed. With Di being as excited as he was at the prospect of finally reaching the magic age of seven that had to be pretty early.

When Di awoke on the dawn of his seventh birthday the gift was there waiting on his bed. Perhaps it would be better to say that it was the gift that woke him up. It wet all over his bed cover. Can I drop all this *it* stuff now ? It was a *HE*, Di's present was a puppy dog. A puppy dog the spitting image of the celebrated Nip in the Nip and Fluff kindergarten best seller.

Di's yell of delight could be heard three streets away, it scared the little dog silly and he tinkled all over the bed for a second time. Mum was not amused and Di had to begin his birthday with a bath.

The incontinent pooch was lucky not to be out on its ear right there and then. Mum had to strip and wash all the bedding with no automatic washing machine in those days. Of course we all called him Nip but within a couple of days it had been extended to Nipper. For the next thirteen years that dog was at the centre of our lives. Wherever we went he went as well, decked in a white ribbon he even came to my wedding. But all that came much later and not until after a lot of water had passed under the proverbial bridge.

While he may have survived that first morning and the wetting of Di's bed there were doubts if he would make it very much further. In anticipation of his joining our little family Mum had laid in a store of tinned dog food. There were several varieties but on that first day he stubbornly refused to eat a thing. Neither would he drink anything that was offered.

"There must be something wrong with him," Mum observed.

"Perhaps he just isn't hungry."

"But he must be," Di pushed a finger into the gooey splodge and offered it up to Nipper. He turned away. "Go on, you must eat something," he insisted, shoving the finger into the animal's mouth. Nipper, true to his name, nipped Di's finger then proceeded to spit out the food all over the kitchen floor. I don't know if you have ever seen a dog spit, it's more like a sneeze, but it spread a small finger of dog food a very long way. The washing of the bed clothes then had to stop to enable the washing of the kitchen floor. It was washed a second time when Di trod in the saucer of milk put down to tempt Nipper.

By lunch time Mum was thinking a visit to the vet may be a good idea. I never was certain if it was to discuss the animal's diet or to have the troublesome creature put down. It was Gran who saved the day.

Di had a birthday tea that afternoon. As well as all his friends both Gran and Great-Aunt Gladys came along to join in the fun. Once he had been shown off Nipper was relegated to then kitchen while the wrapping paper was furiously torn from the packages brought by his many friends. He was kept well out of the way when the jelly and blancmange hit the table. Over the washing up Mum discussed the animal's future with her mother-in-law.

"I am worried about him, I just can't get him to eat a thing."

Gran picked him up, cuddled him and kissed the top of his head. Nipper responded looking into her face. A bond was established that was to last for the rest of his life.

"Richard, get me a slice of bread and butter would you please."

I was there helping with the washing of the jelly plates and sweeping up of cake crumbs. As well as being able to avoid the hilarity of a seven year old's party games in the front room there was also the chance to nick the odd chocolate biscuit that Di and his fellow gannets had missed. There were plenty of sandwiches left which Mum was packing up for Dad's lunches next week. I took one of them and peeled the top slice of bread away from the corned beef below and offered it to Gran.

"Cut it up into little squares will you please Richard."

I did as I was told.

"Now you're going to have some birthday tea as well like a good little doggie. Yes you are, yes you are." She cooed away into Nipper's ear. "You don't want to have to go to the nasty old vet do you ? You want to grow up to be a nice strong doggie don't you." Yuk what soppy talk !

Nipper never did grow much bigger changing little from his puppy days, the canine equivalent of Peter Pan, but that day my Grandmother cured once and for all his refusal to eat. She offered up one small square of bread and butter. Nipper sniffed it, cautiously then took it from Gran's fingers and bolted it whole. His eyes looked about for a second bite. It went down whole in just the same way as the first. Then a third, a fourth, a fifth and a sixth until it was all gone. I pulled a second slice from the sandwich, that week Dad had several sandwiches in his daily lunch box with only one slice of bread, and cut it up as before. When Nipper had eaten his fill it was all washed down with a saucer of milk.

Mum's emotions were mixed, she was pleased of course that Di's birthday present wasn't going to pop its clogs before the day was out but didn't enthuse at being shown up by her mother-in-law. "You obviously weren't doing it properly my dear," she had said. I don't think Mum ever forgave Nipper.

Nipper was supposed to be a Cairn Terrier, as I have already explained he never grew to his full size, but looking at pictures of the breed I can not easily recognise him. He had the funniest face I have ever seen on an animal, not a trace of symmetry anywhere, his left ear pricked up with the right folded over and flopping as he walked. Pointed snout ending in a little black nose and white whiskers. Coat of a dozen shades of brown together with streaks of white. His tail ended as a short s tub which when wagged looked as if it would shake off his bottom entirely. All in all, he was quite a deformed little mutt.

When he first joined our little family everybody wanted to take him off for walkies, in fact it is a wonder his legs weren't worn down to the knees. But as the years went by we were never quite so keen. Fortunately we had a large garden so all that had to be done when we were feeling lazy was to open the back door and Nipper could go out and satisfy the call of nature whenever he felt so inclined. Dad used to huff about the little messages he left behind but then he knew where the lead hung on the back of the kitchen door just as well as anyone.

Nipper, of course, also knew exactly where the lead was kept. He would jump and worry away at it. he could never manager to pull it down. In time scratches appeared alongside, they were painted over and reappeared many times. In all those years

Nipper never managed to pull the lead off the hook but it became something of a ritual.

The lead business wasn't the only ritual old Nipper developed over the years. There was the cheese. This took pace each and every night. Without fail at eight o'clock. Or there about, Nipper would lay on the floor resting his head on Dad's foot. For the next hour he would refuse to budge. If Dad ever attempted to get out of his chair Nipper would clutch his trouser bottom in his teeth and drag behind him. At nine o'clock Dad would say, "Oh well you boys, time for bed." That was the signal. Nipper would sit up and wait. Dad would go to the kitchen, cut two small slices of cheese and that was Nipper's supper. It was absolutely impossible to get away without giving him supper. No way !

Now this was fine when Di and I were little but as we got older our bedtime got later and Nipper's biological clock just could not compensate. So right up until the time I left home I was always told to go off to bed promptly at nine o'clock.

Di's seventh birthday present certainly changed our lives although not the way they were to unexpectedly change when someone else came to live with us. But that's another story and one I'll tell you later. For his eighth birthday Di got that Dan Dare Radio Station. It was his pride and joy for all of a week, was then relegated to the bedroom cupboard and ended up at the church jumble sale.

It was a jumble sale that made me think of Old Nipper who sadly left us for Doggie Heaven many years ago now. I was sorting through some old junk my wife is always threatening to bin when I came across that book: Nip and Fluff. *Here is Nip. Nip is a dog.* I read through it silently from cover to cover, twice. I am not ashamed to admit it brought a tear to my eye.

You were good were you not, you did pick up Nipper's tiepoo and put it in the provided bins ! **Beppo.**

FOOTBALL HOOLIGAN:
I'm a knock-kneed chicken. I'm a bow-legged hen,
Aint had a fight since I don't know when.
I walk with a wiggle and a giggle and a squawk.
I am a Holt End boot boy !

Guide us through the First Division,
Lead us through the dangerous way.
Let us triumph o're Man United,
Lead us to the Tottenham fray.
Aston Villa, Aston Villa,
We'll support you ever more.
We'll support you ever more.

Easy ! Easy !

"Give it a rest Di !"

Where's your father ?
Where's your father ?
Where's your father referee ?
Ain't got one,
Aint got one,
You're a ….

"Enough Di !"

The goalie is a puff,
The goalie is a puff.
Ee aye addio,
The goalie is a puff !

Do you think you could just possibly guess that Di was a football supporter ? Well if you call supporting Aston Villa supporting football that is. Aston Vanilla, the team everybody licks ! It was the unlikely person of Gran who started it all off.

Before you begin imagining a white haired old lady on the terraces, football rattle in hand and scarf about her neck it wasn't like that at all. I doubt of my Grand had ever been to football game in her life, not even in the distant days of her youth but then the was the world's greatest expert on the football pools. Everything stopped in her house on a Saturday afternoon when the classified results came on the television. It was one Saturday when Mum and Dad were to be out late so Di, Nipper and I were sleeping at Grans.

At about five to five she demanded absolute silence, put her reading glasses on and sat, pen in hand, in front of the TV with a strange sheet of paper.

"What's that for Gran ?"

"Tell you later Di now be quiet it's nearly time."

Time for what Gran ?"

"Quiet Di."

"But.."

"Di, be quiet !"

Blackburn Rovers 2	Arenal 1
Birmingham City 0	Nottingham Forrest 1
Luton T own 3	Crystal Palace 2
Oxford United 2	Aston Villa 2
Tottenham Hotspurs 3	Derby County 0

Norwich City 0	Manchester United 2
Liverpool 3	Leyton Orient 1
Manchester City 2	Newcastle 2
Stoke City 1	Everton 3

And so it went on. We sat in reticence while Gran scribbled the results on the copy coupon of her football pools. It was like a religion to her. Monday morning she would take the week's forecast to the post office, buy a postal order and send the lot off to Littlewoods. She never won a big dividend but over the season she always managed several small pay outs making it a reasonably profitable hobby for her. I do remember that week she won fifteen shillings.

Shillings ? Of course some of you won't know what shillings were. You see once upon a time we used to have a different sort of money in this country to that we have today. The pound was still the same although it was a pound note then and not the silly brass coin we all have today. There were twenty shillings in each pound, a shilling being worth five of today's pence, and twelve pennies in a shilling. So a - penny in those days was worth, now let me see – twelve pennies in a shilling times twenty shillings to the pound equals two hundred and forty which means by modern reckoning and old penny was worth ? Hang on I need a calculator. Point four-one-six-six-six-six-six-six P. There was also the half-penny coin, pronounced ha-pen-ey, which would have been worth point two-five- three-three-three-three-three-three-three P. Although they had gone out of use by the time I was born there used to be a farthing, or quarter of a penny which would have been worth – Oh you work it out !

Confused ? Then just hang on a minute longer will you. There were four crowns to the pound and eight half-crowns, each crown worth five shillings and each half-crown worth two shillings and six pence. In silly money today that is twelve and a half pee ! A florin was two shillings or ten pee ! A shilling was known as a *bob* and a six penny piece a *tanner* or a *kick*. So two and a kick or two shillings and six pence or in today's silly money twelve and a half pee. A Guinee was one pound one shilling, one pound ten pee. It was the posh people who used Guinees.

Now what has all that got to do with winning the football pools ? Not a lot but at least you've learned something from English history. Don't ask me what good it will be to you but that's not my problem is it !

Back to Gran's football pool divi. Fifteen shillings, or twenty five pee, was worth something in those days before a succession of incompetent governments invented inflation. Once the results were over Di began to quiz her on the subject of football.

You may think that a young boy should not have been ignorant of our national game but at Banners Gate County Primary School there were only two men teachers, women couldn't possibly teach football it would have been unthinkable. Mr Lloyd was a cricketer and Mr Sullivan, *Sulligogs*, the deputy head had far more important things to do than teach small boys how to chase a ball about a games field. Di's education was about to be completed.

Part of Gran's winnings were set aside and Uncle George, Great Aunt Glady's unmarried son, was detailed off to take Di to Villa Park the next Saturday. In those days Villa Park had a capacity of eighty-two thousand. I have been there with that number – what an atmosphere, and it was anticipated a near capacity crowd would be in attendance for the local derby against Birmingham City. Gran had the game down as a home win, it was up to Di and Uncle George to see they did not let her down.G

Uncle George called round for Di at midday. I don't know what had come over me but I decided I wanted to go as well, so we all walked down the road to catch the 29A corporation 'bus which stopped at the bottom of Trinity Road. It was just over a mile to walk from the 'bus stop to the ground, the entire distance was a river of claret and blue flowing towards Villa Park. The police were directing the Birmingham fans in from Wittan Road so not a blue and white scarf in sight. The air was full of chants: *Villa, Villa, Villa !*

Uncle George usually stood behind the goal in the massive Holt End but Gran insisted he didn't take we children into the crush. The Wittan End was reserved for away supporters and old men so we were going into the Trinity Road stand where we found spaces on the half way line adjacent to the trainer's bench and just below the directors' box. We took up our places nearly two hours before kick off but already the ground was filling quickly.

BBC outside broadcast vans and camera crews indicated the game would be the match that evening on television. Loudspeakers boomed out the latest pop music but were drowned by the singing of the crowd. Some of their word were, well, downright rude and Di memorised every line.

In less than the preceding week Mum had managed to knit us both scarfs in the famous claret and blue Villa colours. We held them out between our outstretched arms and swayed in time to the singing. Occasional chants were heard from the opposing fans but they were soon shouted down, out and into oblivion.

Gran's pool win did not stretch to programmes but Uncle George generously put his hand in his pocket and forked out for us to have a copy each. Di was as happy as a dog with four lampposts.

The pre match noise of the crowd doubled, no trebled, as the teams ran out onto the pitch. Beneath cheers of *Villa, Villa* I do not see how ever they heard the referee's whistle order for the start of play.

After so many years I can not honestly remember all that much detail of the actual match and want to take care not to drift off into a work of fiction. I haven't a clue who scored the goals but do clearly remember by half-time the noise of the Villa supporters had died away somewhat. To compensate the Birmingham fans had discovered their voices. With a score line of Aston Villa 1 Birmingham City 3 it was hardly surprising. Half-time was an air of doom and gloom. Uncle George hardly said a word, heaven help the people at work next Monday morning, he would be unbearable and Great-Aunt Gladys was in for a bad week-end.

The manager must have given the team a terrible talking to back in the dressing room at half time, they pulled back a goal direct from the kick off.

Aston Villa 2 Birmingham City 3

The crowd decided it was about time it spoke up again.

Aston Villa, Aston Villa
We'll support you ever more
We'll support you ever more

The Birmingham fans were having none of that so countered with:

City ! City ! City !

The equaliser came about ten minutes from full time and was followed by the fiercest battle imaginable.

Aston Villa 3 Birmingham City 3

I wasn't paying that much attention at the time, I guess I was thinking about going home, but the call of "Penalty !" and the sheer ecstatic delight when the referee agreed brought me right back into the game.

Villa lined up for the shot. We heard the manager shout from the trainer's bench, "Chico take it." Chico Hamilton was standing just a few yards away from us waiting out on the wing.

"Go to it Chico," Di called, "you show em ! I've got my fingers crossed for you." Chico Hamilton turned and looked at Di, gave him the thumbs up then trotted to the penalty spot. "Good luck," Di screamed after him.

"He'll need it," Uncle George said joining Di in crossing his own fingers. "By my watch it's full time."

A hush descended over Villa Park, every Villa fan praying that Chico wouldn't miss and every City fan praying he would. They may have lost the two goal lead but a draw away at Villa Park would still be a triumph.

Chico Hamilton placed the ball, looked back again in our direction and waved, paced his run up, drew breath and moved in. Just before the kick he kind of shuffled a half-step and whacked a left footed shot into the back of the net. It cannoned past the poor City keeper who, anticipating a right footed attack, dived totally in the wrong direction. He had hardly picked himself up to face the humiliation when the final whistle blew.

The crowd too up with: *Chico – Chico – Chico.* His fellow players mobbed him but he was pushing his way towards the crowd where we were standing.

"Where's my lucky mascot ?" He called looking at Di.

"Me ?" Di shouted in reply.

"You fellows pass him down," Chico ordered.

Di was lifted high and passed over the heads of the crowd until he was set down on the pitch. In those days, of course, there were no fences, just a low wall between supporters and the pitch. Chico swung Di high onto his shoulders before running a lap of honour with him bouncing up and down and waving as if he was royalty. The crowd loved it. So did the TV producer who had the cameras pan round after them.

Uncle George began to chant. "We're going to win the league, we're going to win the league. Ey-ay-addio, we're going to win the league."

"That's my nephew out there you know."

Those about him took up the call and passed it on to others until every Aston Villa fan in the entire stadium was cheering. "We're going to win the league, we're going to win the league. Ey-ay-addio, we're going to win the league."

Villa didn't win the league that season, it was another twenty odd years before they did, but right there and then, thanks to Chico Hamilton and my Brother Di, Aston Villa was totally invincible.

"Would the parents of the young supporter on Chico Hamilton's shoulders please pick him up from the player's dressing room once the team has left the pitch," the tannoy barked out.

Well how about that !

When eventually we managed to find our way to the dressing rooms and persuade the stewards that we had permission to pick up Di the players were in the bath. The room was a fog of steam from the communal bath.

"Richard, Uncle George over here."

Di was in the bath with the entire team, everyone of them modestly wearing a pair of swimming trunks. Where did they find a pair small enough to fit Di ?

"What on earth are you doing in there ?" I asked. "Mum will kill you."

"I'm with my friends."

Chico Hamilton waded across the pool to Uncle George. He reached out and pumped him with a sopping wet handshake. "I was so scared when the Boss shouted for me to take the penalty and then this young man called after me giving me just the confidence I needed."

"We showed 'em Chico didn't we ?"

"We certainly did my young friend. We saved the game and the honour of the best football team in the city."

Uncle George was kind of proud but felt awkward crashing into the privacy of the dressing room, least ways before any of them could put on clothes other than claret and blue swimming trunks.

"I think we'd best be off and out of your way, there'll be massive queues for the 'buses."

"No, let me give you a lift," Chico insisted. "It's the least I can do, I owe you. Here you dry him off while I get ready. He lifted Di dripping water and offered him to Uncle George. "You can use one of the club towels over there. I don't know where he put his clothes but they are about somewhere."

We all got to ride home in Chico Hamilton's car. I expected it to be a Jaguar at the very least but it turned out to be a mini ! Actually a blue and white Mini. He dropped us off at Gran's house where Uncle George had left his car. Gran complained that we didn't have money to waste coming home by taxi.

"But he is one of the footballers," Di protested. He told her all about the game, about Chico Hamilton, about the penalty, about the victory lap and about the communal bath.

"Sounds disgusting to me," she replied. "You'd think a club the size of Aston Villa would be able to afford separate baths for its players ! I shall mark them down for losing on next week's pools coupon."

Toepin the clown here: A bit of a challenge for you and with my being a clown a FUN challenge: *WCJJI* – I want you to detypo that word. Have a go and I'll help you after Di Central Eating has finished his next wild adventure.

THE GREAT TROLLEY RACE:

I was one of the best trolley riders at Banners Gate County Primary School and had dreams of following in the footsteps of Stirling Moss or Mike Hawthorn. My arch rival trolley rider was my best friend Jim, some days I would win the race while on others Jim was the victor. About as much effort went into arguing who was the best as did go into the actual races. Our heated discussions extended far beyond mere wooden trolleys with pram wheels and onto anything at all to do with motorised transport.

"My Dad's got a better car than your Dad's got !"

"Well my Dad's a better driver than your Dad !"

"The just you wait until I am old enough to drive,"

It wasn't all that long since the first motorway in the country had opened, The M1. We planned that for a day this new stretch of road would be closed to all traffic, Jim would take his Dad's car and would take my Dad's, we'd then race all the way to London and back. That would prove once and for all who was the best trolley rider but until the Ministry of Transport could be persuaded to close its newest stretch of road we had to do battle via the more traditional trolley races.

I had owned my trolley for simply ages, Dad had helped me make it when I was really quite small. I had collected four wheels from the yard of the local rag and bone man and Dad had them fitted to axels by the welder at his work. One was fitted to the rear of the trolley that was itself constructed out of four floor boards nailed side by side with solid wooden slats. The whole affair tapered at the front to which was fastened the steering bar and the front pair of wheels. We had heated up a poker in the lounge fire until it was red hot then burned holes through the steering bar and nose of the trolley. A heavy coach bolt held it all together and permitted the steering bar to swivel.

Until such time as Jim and I could test our skill in the ultimate M1 race we devised all kinds of minor trials to evaluate the other's ability at trolley driving. There were three ways to drive a trolley: *Belly Down Bum Up* where the rider lay flat along the length of the vehicle placing his hands direct on the front axel bar so causing the least wind resistance. *Look No Hands* was the trickiest way of all, the rider had to sit with his feet on the steering bar, fold his arms across his chest and use only his legs. The third way was to tie a rope to each side of the front axle and steer *Donkey Derby* by pulling the way it was desired to go. Each and every test had to be undertaken using all three methods.

Jim set out five empty bake bean tins in a line along the footpath at the front of the house. The test was to steer one's trolley between each without hitting any. First donkey derby then belly up bum down and finally look no hands. I successful completed the test.

"Now you have to do it in reverse," Jim chuckled.

I doubted if Jim would be able to do it himself, his trolley had big rear wheels that would be certain to clip the tins, but he was the challenger and I the challenged, the rules said I had to go first.

One of my challenges was an adaptation of the emergency stop from the adult driving test. We each fitted brakes to our trollies in the form of a single length of stout wood screwed to the side. When the handle, or top, of the wood was pushed forward that beneath the pivot jammed against the rear wheel stopping the trolley. If you could get enough speed up and rammed the brake on sharply enough it was possible to skid leaving rubber tyre marks on the pavement. The test was to see who make the longest skid marks.

Of course the only real test of skill was speed. We used to drag our trollies up to the top of Sutton Oak Road and the brow of the steepest hill in the district. The road itself was always heavy with traffic but the pavement was normally void of pedestrians. So this became our number one grand prix circuit. Some days I would be the fastest and on others Jim would come first.

There were, of course, other trolley riders besides Jim and I but they were decidedly second division material. Keith, for example, rode such a ramshackled old heap that it was a miracle it went along at all. Steven was posh so never called his trolley an trolley, it was a go-kart. What nonsense, who did he think he was ? Snob ! And then there was Di.

Dad made Di a trolley giving in to his incessant whining over a period of several weeks. It was modelled on my own but a little shorter and not quite so heavy. I tried it out on Sutton Oak Hill but I was far too used to my own machine so did not like it very much. Di's novice skill at driving coupled with the trolley's smaller design would never see him as a threat to the domination of the sport by Jim and myself. With a little care I made two "L" plates out of white card and red crayon, fixing the front and back of Di's trolley. He thought it funny but he would then wouldn't he.

It was Jim who decided upon the Great Trolley Race, The Sutton Oak Hill Grand Prix. Racing would be by invitation only, each contestant would pay an entry fee of two shillings with the winner scooping the lot. Of course Jim and I would be there, one of us after all was going to be the winner. Keith was invited, just so there was somebody to come last and Steven with his go-kart making four of us.

"Pity we can't find another driver," Jim observed, "just to get the winnings up to ten bob."

Ten bob ? What I could do with ten bob. It was a small fortune. "There's always Di," I explained. Now whatever made me say that ?

Jim pondered, would it be fair ? Di lacked experience but then his entry fee would make up the winnings. He agreed to the invitation being offered and I was instructed to sign him on. I would do it that evening after tea.

The next job was to decide upon the rules. It wouldn't be possible to race five trollies down the hill at the same time, the pavement wasn't wide enough. What was needed was some kind of time trial. Jim tore a sheet out of his English exercise book and we sat down to work out details. Each trolley rider would race down Sutton Oak Hill three times, once in each of the three approved riding positions. Times would be kept for individual laps then added together against each driver, the one with the lowest figure would be the winner and receive the ten shillings.

"Who's going to keep time ?" I asked.

"It'll have to be someone who's impartial, not one of the five riders I mean."

"It'll have to be someone who can add up as well," I said. "We can't afford any mistakes with so much prize money at stake."

"How about Mickey Turner, he's brilliant at maths and his Dad's a football referee ?"

"What's a football referee got to do with it ?"

"Football referees have stop watches don't they so he could borrow it and use it to keep time."

"Do you fancy asking Old Man Turner if he'd let us use his best football referee's stop watch to time a trolley race ?"

Mickey didn't either. His dad had a terrible temper and was known as the grumpiest parent at Banners Gate County Primary School. However, Mickey agreed that if we made it worth his while he would sneak it out, do the timing then put it back before his Dad was any the wiser.

"What do you mean, make it worth your while ?"

"You pay me half a crown to do the job," Mickey explained.

"Half a crown ! That would mean our prize money would have to be cut to seven and six. What do you think Richard ?"

I already had the answer. "I say we put the entry fee up to two and six from two bob, that'll get Mickey his half-crown."

"Good thinking." So that was organised.

It was at the next day that Mickey came up with a problem. "You can't see the top of the hill from the bottom," he explained, "so I won't be able to time things properly. I won't be able to see the start and set the watch."

"How about standing half way and watching the start and the finish from there ?" I suggested.

"No good, I thought of that," he replied. "In the middle you can't see either the top or the bottom, the hill's too steep."

I suppose you could always ride down with each driver and time them that way," Jim offered.

"What about wind resistance ?" I protested.

"Forget about any wind resistance," Mickey protested, "if you think I'd risk my Old Man's stop watch on fifteen trolley dashes down Sutton Oak Hill you must be off your head. It'd be sure to get busted and he'd knock me into the middle of next week !"

Um, we had a problem right enough and one the best mathematician and the two best trolley riders in the school could not solve.

"If only I'd had that Dan Dare Radio Station for my birthday," Di said when I told him the race looked like being called off."

"But what use would a Dan Dare Radio Station be ?" I have to confess in spite of my interest in interplanetary travel I knew very little about the subject save it being then latest toy designed about the Dan Dare Space stories.

"It's got a walkie talkie set in it. If the starter had the base set at the top of the hill he could tell the time keeper on the remote when he set the trolley off."

You know for a fool my brother was quite clever. "But you didn't get a Dan Dare Radio Station for your birthday did you !"

"No, but Simon Turner did and it's his brother Mickey who's going to be the time keeper so he'd be bound to help."

Simon Turner drove a much harder bargain than did his brother. Not only did he want half a crown to use his Dan Dare Radio Station but he also wanted another half a crown for the batteries. So up went the entry fee to three shillings and six pence. Keith and Snobby Steven protested but paid up in the end. To soften the blow it was agreed that the winner, whoever he turned out to be, would buy the other four an ice cream once the race was over. If I won they'd make do with penny ice-pops, none of your sixpenny Mivi's, I wanted as much of the prize money left intact as possible.

The grand prix was set for the Wednesday afternoon of half-term and every one of us went into strict training. We paid our entry fees to Mickey Turner who would act as judge as well as time keeper. I prepared my trolley for the challenge. I oiled the wheels, greased the steering bolt and practised the entire day before the race. When I got to the hill Jim, Keith and Snobby Steven were already there testing modifications on their own vehicles. Only Did didn't seem to be bothered about things but then it was possible that even Keith would beat him so I guess he could see little point in making any effort before the time of the actual event.

Although Di stuffed his face as usual, ever since his teeth had grown he hadn't stopped eating, I didn't each very much that lunch time. I wanted to be fit and I had this thing about keeping the wind resistance down, I could not afford to put on weight at the last minute. With the washing up out of the way we took up the steering ropes of our trolleys and dragged them to the foot of Sutton Oak Hill.

The other drivers were already there as were the Turner Brothers. Mickey had his Dad's stop watch and Simon the Radio Station with, I trust, a new set of batteries. Jim had written the names of all the drivers on slips of paper then folded them up. He offered them to Mickey to draw out the race order. Jim, himself, was to go first, then Keith, me third, Snobby Steven fourth and Di last. We agreed it didn't matter which order each driver chose to race the three styles. I has kind of decided to start with look no hands, then donkey derby and to keep belly down and bum up for my last descent of the hill but I would wait and see what the others did.

We walked to the top of the hill pulling the trolleys behind us, the Turner Brothers checked the radio link. It crackled, after all it was only a toy or perhaps the batteries needed replacing (I bet he had pocketed that extra half a crown rather than use it on batteries) but it worked well enough. Jim moved to the start line and selected the belly down bum up stance, flattening himself against the wood of his trolley, trying to mould to its shape. The starter began the count down.

"Ready Jim, after five then. Five – four – three – two – one – OFF !"

Jim gave a kick to start the trolley moving then four more as it gathered momentum. We all watched as he sped towards the bottom. It may not have been possible to see the top from the bottom but you could certainly see the bottom from the top. We watched him all the way down.

"Twenty-five point two seconds," Mickey crackled over the Dan Dare Radio Station. Although we had never before times our races down Sutton Oak Hill we knew it was a pretty good time.

By comparison Keith took an age using the look no hands method.

"Fifty-one seconds dead," Mickey reported.

Me next. I decided to stick with my plan to do the same as Keith with look no hands, I was certain to better his time. I took my place, settled into position making myself as comfortable as possible. I felt a heavy pair of hands on my back to push me off.

"Five – four – three – two – one – OFF !" A fierce shove and down I started.

I began counting in my head, I just had to beat Keith although riding that was I knew I could not overtake Jim's leading time, my chance would come in the final round. Twenty-three, twenty-four, twenty-five, the descent was taking forever, twenty-six, twenty-seven, twenty-eight. How long had Keith taken ? Fifty-one seconds ? I had to beat Keith's time. Twenty-six, twenty-seven, I'd said that before, twenty-seven, twenty-seven. Come on, come on I had to beat Keith. Where was the finish line ? It looked miles away. Come on, come on, come on !

"How long ? How long ?" Once past Mickey I jumped off, grabbed the trolley and screamed again. "Mickey how long ?"

"Forty-nine point three."

"Forty-nine point three, I'd beaten Keith but only just. I'd have to do better in the next round.

I waited at the bottom of the hill to note the times of Steven and Di. Steven used the fast belly down method and achieved a time of thirty-two point seven seconds while Di rode Donkey Derby and a time of thirty-one point two. So the position after first round was Jim first, Di second. Di second ?, Steven third, me fourth and Keith, as anticipated, last. Even using the slow no hands style I was not pleased with my performance.

At the end of the second round I was still in fourth position, the only satisfaction came from Di slipping back to third place. Jim had lost his lead to Snobby Steven and Keith was still coming in last. For the final round Keith, Di and I were all to ride belly down, Jim was finishing with donkey derby and Steven look no hands, Mickey Turner had added up the total times.

Snobby Steven   67.4 seconds
Jim   75 .0 seconds
Di Central Eating   78.8 seconds
Me   82.5 seconds
Keith   86.4 seconds

I tried to calculate the time I would have to achieve if I was going to win, then I tried to work out what I needed to avoid coming last. I couldn't come last, I should be the winner or at the very, very least runner up. My brain ached with the mathematical calculations but there were too many variable or perhaps it was just that I wasn't good enough at adding up.

So there we were at the top of Sutton Oak Hill shivering with excitement as the final round began. As with the other two races Jim went first. Riding donkey derby he crouched low clutching the steering rope. Every eye watched every inch of the descent then every breath was held as we awaited he official time from Mickey Turner. Thirty-four point seven, that was a slow time for a donkey derby, my own had been thirty-two point six.

"That gives a total race time," Mickey's voice came over the Dan Dare Radio Station, "of one-o-nine point seven."

My time so far was eighty-two point five. I attempted the maths again, which meant I would have to make the belly down run in under twenty-seven point two to beat Jim. That shouldn't be too difficult, Keith made his belly down run in thirty-one point two to give him a grand total of one-one-seven point six. Pathetic ! I was next. Twenty-seven point two, I had to beat twenty-seven point two. My heart thumped and the adrenaline flowed, the butterflies in my stomach developed hiccups. Twenty-seven point two.

"Five – four – three – two – one – OFF !"

I stabbed my foot out and started the run. Six times more I scooted the trolley forward until I felt it had reached its maximum speed. Gripping the steering bar like a vice I pressed my body against the wood until they became as one then set my eyes to focus on the finish line at the bottom. There stood Mickey Turner, watch in hand, counting off the seconds. Twenty-seven point two, I had to make it in under twenty-seven point two. This time I hadn't started counting in my head, I just hoped I was making good enough speed.

The wind blew in my face and I felt it glide over my body, the shirt rippled on my back. Twenty-seven point two, I was sure I was going to make it.

It was all over so quickly, I flashed past Mickey and skidded to a halt some twenty-five yards further on. I didn't get the chance to ask him before he volunteered the information.

"Twenty-eight point nine, Richard." Words of doom, "that gives you a total race time of one eleven point four."

Damn, damn, damn, damn, damn, damn, damn ! I'd missed it. Curses, by one point seven seconds I'd missed it. Jim would win and I would settle for second place. Second place and no ten shilling prize money. I was so fed up I paid little or no attention at all to Snobby Steven's final run. At the end of the second round true enough he was first place but with the final fun in the look no hands position it wasn't possible that he would manage to beat either Jim or myself. I was right, with a time of fifty-one point six he fell right back behind even Keith. Oh well just Di to run down and it would be time for Jim to be confirmed as winner.

Mickey had been right about the camber of the hill. Standing at the bottom it was impossible to see Di start his run although we heard Simon's voice over the Dan Dre hand set say he was on his way. Mickey clicked the watch to start counting, he called the time off every five seconds. He had only just called ten when Di came into view. Like lightening he flashed down the hill. "Fifteen." How he could be so fast on a trolley I could not imagine. I saw his foot reach out and give two quick pushes at the ground, speeding the trolley toward the finish line. "Twenty." Mickey had hardly finished speaking when Di hurtled past us. The watch clicked to a halt.

"Twenty-four point three which gives total of one-o-three point one made makes Di the grand prix winner.

Brother Di the winner ? Not Jim ? Jim pushed into second place by the youngest driver, my brother Di ? Had I really been pushed into third place ? Had Mickey Turner added up the times incorrectly ? No, he produced a sheet of paper with all the times neatly recorded, there was no mistake. Di Central Eating was the winner of the first Sutton Oak Hill Invitation Grand Prix.

Jim offered his congratulations, as did Keith and Snobby Steven. Reluctantly I joined them. Mickey handed over the prize money and we all followed Di to the ice cream shop. He was generous towards us all, including Mickey and Simon in the round. I don't know what he spent the rest of the prize money on but I don't mind telling you that ice cream nearly choked me.

Beppo AGAIN: So did you manage to detypo the word *WCJJI* ?

We clowns use a straightforward alphabet. To remind you:

A B C D E F G H I J K L M N O P Q R S T U V W X Y Z

Uncomplicated enough but not enough for you humans. You are greedy and demand to use two alphabets ! Oh yes you do:

Q W E R T Y U I O P A S D F G H J K L Z X C V B N M

Is it any wonder you are addicted to typo's as you call them.

Let's *DEtypo* WCJJI………

W = B   C = E   J = P   J = P   I = O

There you have it **BEPPO**.

AND THEN WE WERE THREE:
My Mum used to spend most evenings in front of the television, indeed she still does, clicking together knitting needles. Nearly all of our jumpers came from her hobby which had an output to rival the factories of Marks and Sparks. She gave talks on the subject at the Young Wives Club and, although an amateur, she was an acknowledged local expert. Nobody, therefore, to begin with at least paid very much attention to her increased level of production.

I think I was the first to notice there was something out of place. The strange thing was she started using only white wool and the results of her efforts were far too small to fit either Di or myself. Instead they were stored away in an old blue suitcase on top of Mum and Dad's bedroom wardrobe. It didn't make a lot of sense to me.

Di said something about Mum putting on weight but she was always fussing about going on a diet at the time turning enough food out of her kitchen to feed an army.

Ever since he had been born I had shared a bedroom with Brother Di. He was more than a bit of a pest but I got used to his snoring and nightmares, even his collection of teddy bears which was a source of embarrassment every time a friend came into our room. Besides the box room was so full of collected junk it was quite uninhabitable. Then one Saturday Dad instructed us both to help him clear it all out.

"Why are we doing this Dad ?"

"Better ask your mother."

"But she's not here is she ?"

"Where's she gone ?"

"Just popped out to look at some wallpaper."

"Wallpaper ? What does she want wallpaper for ?"

"To put on walls idiot."

The sudden desire to decorate didn't fit in. Dad had only just finished the lounge and the wallpaper in their bedroom was less than a year old.

"Which room are you going to decorate ?"

"This one."

"Why ?"

"You can't expect the baby to sleep in it as it is now."

BABY ! BABY ! What baby ? The secret was out, Mum was expecting a baby ! Jeeps I didn't want another brother, Di was more than enough ! But then what if was a sister, a sister ? Impossible !

Di has always been naïve, he still is, but this was one area of the subject I have to confess I joined him in. To the best of my knowledge babies came from the shops just like everything else. Not shops like those down the road, Ken Riley Hardware or Tom O'Connell's Greengrocery, but big shops up in the town. The department stores like Lewis's or Rackham's, after all when I had been there with Gran I saw them. They had a big sign on the wall: *Baby Department*.

So the box room was duly decorated with soppy infant wallpaper, Great Aunt Gladys sewed up matching curtains and Gran gave Mum five pounds to buy a new carpet. The cot, pram and baby bath both Di and I had used were unpacked from the attic, dusted down and made ready for the baby's arrival.

It was so humiliating when Mum began remembering when we had been little babies and then telling everyone about it. "I do so wish you'd never grown up," she cooed. Daft !

Was that why she wanted another baby ? When that one started to grow up would she want another, and then another ? Where would it end ? How much did babies cost ? Babies from Lewis's would be cheaper than those from Rackham's, Rackham's was where the posh people shopped. I ventured to suggest this to a friend at school who explained that babies were delivered to homes by birds called storks. It was so unlikely I knew he was making it all up.

My little sister, yes it was a girl, was a long time coming. I presume they must have been out of stock at Lewis's. She eventually came along one cold March day. Mum took to her bed and Gran came round to look after us, Neither Di nor I, not even Dad were allowed up there to see her. Later on a lady called the Midwife came round. She had with her a big black bag in which I presume she had the baby. She must have been up to town, to Lewis's to collect it. Babies where back in stock and on the shelves.

When I first saw it, it was bawling its little head off, it was making more noise than even Di could on a good day. I wondered if Lewis's gave refunds but then Mum looked happy so I thought it would not have been fair to send it back.

It was named Anne after the young Princess Anne. Thank goodness Mum and Dad were not that patriotic when I was born, I would hate to have been called Charles.

Pictures of Prince Charles and Princess Anne appeared on special saving stamps which were on sale each week at school. Charles stamps cost half a crown and were blue in colour while Anne's were green and cost just one shilling. Di and I used to be sent to school with a shilling every Friday to buy one of Princess Anne's saving stamps which we suck in a special book. When the book was full we would take it down to the post office and exchange it for a savings certificate which was paced in a bank book. Years later we cashed them in and transferred the money to an organisation called Barclays but that's another story.

"I hope she don't grow up to look like those saving stamps," Do observed, "'cos she's dead ugly." True the picture of Princess Anne was hardly flattering but he should learn to keep his mouth shut. People have ended up in The Tower of London for saying less.

"Your new sister in every was is a princess in her own right," Gran said but neither of us knew what she meant by that. Perhaps she'd marry Prince Charles.

Dad leaned over and kissed his new daughter, then he kissed Mum. "Well done darling, she's perfect." What did he mean, well done ? Mum hadn't done very much. After all it was the midwife that had been up town to buy her, all Mum had done was to stay in bed.

If Di was the perfect pest of brother then Anne was double so as a sister and yet I loved her so very much. When Mum first let me hold her I went all tingly and the hair stood up on the back of my neck. The smell of talcum powder and baby cream was sweet even if Di said it stank. I'm not quite sure if I could say I loved her so much when she exercised her lungs in the middle of the night but as she grew up Anne and I became very close indeed. As I had done before her, she found pronouncing David almost impossible. Just as well we called him Di. But it was simply ages before she could manage Central Eating.

Life is a Typo – if you don't make any then you are not living it fast enough. Who said that ? DAVID said that.

Life is a lot more fun if you are a little bit silly. (Silly NOT stupid) Who said that ? Beppo of course.

Time now for Di's very last adventure, but is it an adventure and is it Di who is having it ?

THE GYPSY'S CURSE:
NOW HANG ON A MINUTE !

Just stop right there will you ! This is David Albon writing now, not that fool of a brother of mine who thinks he is the next Enid Blyton or Roald Dhal. What's this all about – Wild Adventures ? Fish and platinum plated pitchforks ? You don't honestly believe all that rubbish do you ?

Do you ?

Pardon, what did you say ?

I thought so !

Now let's be realistic shall we. Brother Richard may be one of the most prolific writers of his time but nobody ever reads any of his scribble. I know he's got dreams of fame and fortune but William Shakespeare he is not. Let's face it he hasn't ever had so much as a full stop published. But, just in case, just in case someone is fool enough to pick up the manuscript and have nothing better to do than read it I would like to set the record straight.

My name is David Albon, yes OK then Di Central Eating if you like but nobody's called me that for years. If Richard doesn't watch out I'll tell you what we used to call him. What the heck why not, you'd like to know wouldn't you ? *Dickie-Dirt,* that's what we used to call him. Dickie-Dirt ! Dickie because it's short for Richard and Dirt, well that was my Mother's idea. Richard, you see, was allergic to water, at least when it was mixed with soap. He certainly was a scruffy kid, I wish some of his posh friends of today could have seen him then.

Dickie-Dirt, what a cheek to sit down and here expose all my childhood secrets. I'll get him, you wait and see if I don't, I'll stitch him up. So what can I tell you about him ? What dark secrets can I reveal ? There was the grasshopper hopper he put in Mum's teapot and the time he baked a cake for the school hobbies exhibition, the teacher who judged the competition was taken into hospital with food poisoning. Then there was the time when he got drunk on Dad's home brew and slept it off in the garden shed before anyone found out. There you are Mum and Dad, you never knew about that did you !

Well if daft Brother Dickie-Dirt can tell you about my dreams of being a pop star or making pretend voyages into space then I can tell you about the gypsy's curse. So sit down, pin back your lug holes and cop a load of this !

To this very day Brother Richard, sorry I mean Dickie-Dirt, has a phobia about frogs. Yes, those little jumpy things you find at the edges of ponds. It's not that he doesn't like them or is even scared of them, more accurately he is terrified. At the very sight he becomes physically sick and his whole body turns to a quivering wreck. He once applied for a job with MI5 but was turned down on account of this fear. It seemed they thought all the enemy would have to do would be to wave a frog under his nose for Dickie to reveal every state secret ever known to mankind. Last summer he found a frog in his garden, it wasn't doing very much just sitting there sunning itself but it sent him into cardiac arrest. His two sons had to go and catch it, put it in a dustbin bag and then his wife had to drive it ten miles away and release it. He refused to go back into the garden for nearly a week and cancelled a barbecue he was hosting for ten business customers. All because of the gypsy's curse.

I don't remember how old we were at the time but it must have been before Dad contracted the Percy Thrower bug for our garden was something of a jungle. Dickie and I were playing in the undergrowth pretending to be Tarzan or something similar. It wasn't much of a game, Dickie always wanted to direct the play never letting me be the hero and never playing the way I wanted to. It was some time during the school holidays because we had been playing all morning and intended to continue after lunch. Mum was in the kitchen cooking, Mum was always in the kitchen cooking, and Dad was out at work. It was before Anne invaded our lives, did you read what he wrote about her ? Where she came from I mean – Lewis's Baby Department ! I ask you, what a prize pillock ! Anyway, there we were stalking some ferocious beast. Armed with poison tipped spears we were set on sending it to the hereafter so saving all the surrounding native villages from its nightly reign of terror. No more would the people fear their children being carried off, no longer would the shepherd lose his flock to the foul beast that came with the darkness.

We were slashing our way through the undergrowth when the foul beast jumped right in front of Dickie. It threw itself at him, slapping its body against his lower leg. Fearless Tarzan flung down his spear and bolted for the safety of the house.

"Mummy, Mummy there's a frog in the garden !"

I did not follow him immediately but instead continued to stalk the creature, I had other plans. It was easy to track him down and easy to capture him. I held the evil brute of the forest in my two hands and followed Dickie into the house.

Mum had left the kitchen and was at the front door talking to a gypsy woman who was trying to sell lace table covers and wooden clothes pegs. You don't see that sort of thing these days, Romanies are more interested in scrap cars and other metals, but when we were children it was quite common for their women folk to peddle their wares door to door. Mum was just wondering if one of the lace table covers would make a suitable birthday present for Great Aunt Gladys when Dickie burst in, still shouting he clutched at Mother's skirts.

"Mummy, mummy there's a frog in the garden," he continued to blurt, "it jumped right at me." The shock has quite un-nerved him.

Mum was obviously quite embarrassed. "Don't be so silly Richard, stop all that noise, besides it's gone now."

"No it aint Mum," I made my entrance, "I caught it and here it is." I offered it up for Dickie to look at. He screeched hiding behind Mum's back."

"Di take it away," she ordered. "Put it back in the garden." I tossed it out the front door past the gypsy woman where it landed on the path and sat there.

"Make it go away Mummy, please make it go away," Dickie pleaded.

Bravely I went outside, put my toe behind it and helped it on its way. The animal hopped off into the road. Just then a car came past and splattered it. To a seven year old it was lovely, guts spewed all over the tarmac. At nine years of age, however, Dickie did not appreciate it and continued his hysterical screaming.

"I'm so sorry about all this," Mum apologised, "please don't go away I want to buy one of those lovely lace covers. I'll just get my purse."

"No hurry Dearie," the old woman smiled, "and don't worry. Come here my little man, let the old gypsy lady take away your troubles."

Dickie didn't know if he was more scared of a gypsy than he was of the frog but fear is a great motivator, terror is even better. He did as he was told as Mum pushed him off her to go and find her purse. The gypsy woman smiled. "He can't hurt you now, his body's dead and the spirit of animals never hurt anyone. What makes you so frightened ?"

"It was horrible," Dickie sobbed, "all jumpy and nasty."

"There, there," she soothed, "he didn't mean to frighten you and now the poor little thing is dead."

"But it was horrible."

"I know. What's your name ?"

"Richard."

"Well Richard let the old gypsy lady weave a little magic for you." She placed a hand on Richard's head and closed her eyes.

"There all better now. You'll never lose your fear of frogs Richard but the spirit of this dead frog will watch over you and protect you for the rest of your life."

Mum bought her lace table cloth and the gypsy woman was gone. Before she left she kissed Dickie gently on the cheek. "Now remember what I have said to you Richard."

All mumbo jumbo if you ask me but the fact remains to this day Brother Richard has a nausea ting terror of frogs. Their very sight illogically makes him want to vomit from every inch of his body and yet in all other ways he has been terribly lucky in everything he attempts. I wasn't exactly telling the truth earlier about MI5, all his working life Dickie has run his own business which is fabulously successful. He has a lovely wife, three super kids and all in all he's not a bag guy even if he is my big brother. Perhaps there was something in the gypsy's spell after all, or was it a curse ? Spell for fortune, curse for frogs. I expect the old girl's long dead by now, is her gypsy spirit up there with that of the splattered frog, looking down on all he does and guiding his destiny ? I'm going to put it to the test.

In between business deals Brother Richard likes to write books. This is his ninth full-length novel. I 've hacked into his word processor and pulled out copies of them all. He's never attempted to sell any to a publisher, I guess he's got enough intelligence to realise no sane person would ever want to read any such illiterate scribble. To the end of this manuscript I have now added my own final chapter and fully intend to send copies to a variety of publishing houses. With a certainty each and every one of them will dismiss the opus, so proving the gypsy's spell to be nothing more than a load of baloney. If, however, one takes sufficient leave of its senses to print and distribute such nonsense, if you are reading these words in a small book complete with glossy cover, author's pseudonym, line drawings and ISBN, perhaps purchased from W H Smith's then you will know the gypsy's spell to be true and we'll say no more. Good Bye !

And so ends the adventured of Di Central Eating but Beppo and David have one more adventure before you can close this book and throw it in the recycling bin !

Honeycomb:
For seven decades David and Beppo have been close friends. David is wearing quite well, he still has his own hair and that hair is not grey. Beppo's hair is grey, well make that white, clowns all have hair that is white. As for Beppo's nose, it glows as red as it has ever done.

From Queen Victoria and her little tree to Yuri Gagarin and his life on Mars, from Nipper the Dog to Kit the Kat and that wonderful class teacher Miss Hudson who made everything possible, if you are looking down from the puppet stage in the sky David and Beppo hope you have enjoyed their recalling these chocolate adventures. Time for one more taste of fun.

"How about a Crunchie bar ?" Beppo suggested.

"That's honeycomb," David replied. "You know what, I really quite fancy one."

Oh, what a glorious thing to be
A healthy, grown-up, busy-busy bee
Whiling away the passing hours
Pinching all the pollen from the cauliflowers
I'd like to be a busy-busy bee
Being just as busy as a bee can be
Flying around the garden, sweetest ever seen
Taking back the honey to the dear old queen

"Hello there, I'm Bertie the Bee. Thank you for coming here to visit me in my comb of honey."

"I think it is going to be fun being here," Beppo said.

"I know it is going to be fun being here," David said.

Oh, what a glorious thing to be
A healthy, grown-up, busy-busy bee
Making hay while time is ripe
Building up the honey-comb just like tripe
I'd like to be a busy-busy bee
Being just as busy as a bee can be

"On one of your earlier bites of chocolate, "Bertie buzzed, "you met a certain cat, that's cat spelt with a *T* and not a *K*, by the name of Tigger."

"We did."

"He has a friend by the name of Winnie. That's not Winnie as in Winnie Churchill, you've already met one prime minister and that's more than enough, but Winnie as in Winnie the Pooh. He spells honey, hunny."

"How do you know all this ?"

"Bees are omnipresent, we fly everywhere and anywhere."

"Bees sting people," Beppo suggested.

"Two things," Bertie said in reply. "You are not a people, you are a clown and bees do not sting people. Wasps sting people, bees kiss them."

"If bees don't sting clowns," Beppo said, "then I can go out into the garden at home more than I do. David has a beautiful garden with hundreds and hundreds of flowers."

"It's not me who has the green fingers," David clarified, "but my wife."

"I don't have green fingers," Beppo explained. "Mine are blue but the gloves I wear are white."

"Could your wife perhaps use some help in your garden ?" Bertie hoped for a *yes* in David's answer.

"Definitely !" Was David's *yes*.

"Then maybe she would allow me to help,"

"I am sure that she would."

"On one condition, that you let me give you a honeycomb chocolate bar every day."

Oh, what a glorious thing to be
A healthy, grown-up, busy-busy bee
Whiling away the passing hours
Pinching all the pollen from the cauliflowers
I'd like to be a busy-busy bee
Being just as busy as a bee can be
Flying around the garden, sweetest ever seen
Taking back the honey to the dear Mrs David

BEPPO THE CLOWN AND DAVID HIS FRIEND: A story for children written for grownups to read………….

THE END (Or is it.)

Printed in Dunstable, United Kingdom

70291899R10109